COLLEGE OF ALAMEDA LIBRARY
WITHDRAWN

D0761062

E
467
M115   Macartney, Clarence
             Lincoln and his
         generals.

DATE DUE

MAR 3 '39			
NOV 7 '8			
MAR 17 '88			
MAR 25 '92			

LENDING POLICY
IF YOU DAMAGE OR LOSE LIBRARY
MATERIALS, THEN YOU WILL BE
CHARGED FOR REPLACEMENT. FAIL-
URE TO PAY AFFECTS LIBRARY
PRIVILEGES, GRADES, TRANSCRIPTS,
DIPLOMAS, AND REGISTRATION
PRIVILEGES OR ANY COMBINATION
THEREOF.

MWANGETHE

Lincoln and His Generals
Clarence Edward Macartney

LINCOLN AT ANTIETAM

Reading from left to right, the fourth figure from the end is Major General George W. Morrell; the sixth, facing Mr. Lincoln, Major General George B. McClellan; the twelfth, Major General Fitz John Porter, and the fifteenth, Brigadier General Andrew A. Humphreys.

To the
122,388 Surviving Followers
of
Lincoln and His Generals

Lincoln and His Generals

By

Clarence Edward Macartney

Illustrated with Official Photographs from
the War Department.

 BOOKS FOR LIBRARIES PRESS
FREEPORT, NEW YORK

First Published 1925
Reprinted 1970

STANDARD BOOK NUMBER:
8369-5429-7

LIBRARY OF CONGRESS CATALOG CARD NUMBER:
70-124241

PRINTED IN THE UNITED STATES OF AMERICA

CONTENTS

LIST OF ILLUSTRATIONS

PREFACE

The visitor to Philadelphia's beautiful Fairmount Park will see on a hill overlooking the Schuylkill River a plain board shanty with the United States flag flying over it. It is the cabin used as headquarters by Grant at City Point on the James River, in 1864 and 1865. In that room the orders were written which directed the far flung armies of the nation in the last year of the Civil War. As one passes the cabin it is not difficult to see, in imagination, some of the chief military and political actors of the great drama: the severe and scholarly Meade, the dynamic Sheridan, the "superb" Hancock, the thoughtful Warren, the big and manly Burnside, the restless Sherman, with the fire of genius burning in his eyes, the capable Porter, Grant smoking a cigar, a hand thrust into his pocket, and Lincoln with his high silk hat and frock coat, and melancholy countenance.

Of the making of many books about Lincoln there is no end. But in this book the reader is invited to enter a field which has been little traversed by others. Lincoln as a lawyer, as a politician, as an executive, as a story-teller, as an orator, as a master of men, as a man of sorrows and acquainted with grief, we all know. But there is a side to Lincoln's character which cannot be understood save by a study of his relationships with the chief generals of the Union armies during the war. It is that side which I have tried to bring out in this series of papers. In contrast with Jefferson Davis, who had been trained at West Point, who had served in the Mexican War and had been Secretary of War under President Pierce, Lincoln had no knowledge of military affairs, save a brief and rather farcical experience as captain of a company of volunteers in the Black Hawk War. Most of the officers whom Jefferson Davis appointed to high commands at the beginning of the war continued to occupy places of prominence until its close. But in the United States Army generals were exalted one day only to be put down the next. Until Grant came on the stage as commander-in-chief, nearly every great battle saw a new commander for the Union army engaged.

Major-General W. F. Smith said of Lincoln, "I have long held to the opinion that at the close of the war Mr. Lincoln was the superior of his generals in his comprehension of the effect of strategic movements and the proper methods of following up victories." After Bull Run Lincoln gave himself assiduously to the study of the campaigns and mapped out plans of his own. Neither McClellan nor Grant thought highly of the plans which he submitted to them, and the student of Lincoln's relationships to his generals will hardly hold the high opinion entertained by General Smith. The campaigns with which Lincoln had the most to do were the least successful, and those with which he had the least to do were the most successful. After Grant took supreme command Lincoln gave the details of the campaign little attention, for he felt that he now had what he told Grant he had long been waiting for, a man who would take the responsibility and act. Lincoln told Grant when they first met at Washington that he did not profess to know how to conduct military campaigns, but that the procrastination of former commanders and the pressure from the people and from Congress, always with him, had compelled him to take a hand in military matters and issue orders. He confessed that many of his orders were wrong.

If anyone expects that Lincoln will be held up in these pages as a military genius, adding that crown to the many others already resting upon his brow, he will be disappointed. Lincoln was far from that. But he who would have some fresh view of the infinite patience of Lincoln, the peculiar trials and vexations to which he was subjected, the jealousies and quarrels which hampered him, the Gethsemanes of sorrow and disappointment through which he passed, and his magnificent faith in the nation and in the cause, may be repaid by the reading of this book.

CLARENCE EDWARD MACARTNEY

Lincoln and His Generals

LINCOLN AND SCOTT

History affords few instances of a man so advanced in years bearing such heavy military responsibilities as those which rested on the shoulders of Lieutenant-General Winfield Scott at the outbreak of the Civil War. He was then seventy-five years old, very heavy and unwieldy in body, suffering from a painful affliction of the spine, and for a number of years had been unable to mount a horse. Yet his great age and evident infirmity had not in any way diminished the high regard, and even reverence, in which he was held when the beginning of the conflict made the nation ask itself in whom it could put its confidence. For half a century he had played a great part in the affairs of the nation. Victories such as Lundy's Lane, won in the remote period of the War of 1812, and his more recent successes in the campaign against Mexico, where with a small army of twelve thousand men he conquered a nation, and where his successive victories seemed to revive the memories of Cortez, had won him great military renown both at home and abroad. Nor was he altogether unworthy of this high regard as a soldier and strategist. His Mexican campaign was a splendid piece of military thinking as well as execution, and it has been said that there are few battles where the history of the engagements coincided with the plans and orders of the commander as they did in Scott's battles in Mexico. When the Civil War came, General Scott, although old and infirm, had a far clearer conception of the problems of the war than many a younger officer or statesman. His chief fault was vanity. Grant, who served under him in Mexico, thus refers to this trait: "General Scott was precise in language, cultivated a style peculiarly his own; was proud of his rhetoric; not averse to speaking of himself, often in the third person, and he could bestow praise upon the person he was talking about without the least embarrassment."

In the dark and uncertain months toward the close of Buchanan's administration, Scott understood thoroughly the perilous situation of the United States forts which stood within the states threatening to secede, and urged that measures be taken for their defense. But in this he was balked, partly through the timidity of Buchanan, partly through the treasonable plans of men in his administration, and partly through the lack of means and men. As far back as 1857 Scott had said to Sherman, just returned from California, "The country is on the verge of a terrible civil war." When South Carolina threatened to secede from the Union in 1832 Scott was in command of the forces sent to Charleston by President Jackson, and his experience upon that occasion undoubtedly made him anxious for the outcome of the new agitation. In October, 1860, he submitted to President Buchanan his "Views suggested by the imminent danger of a disruption of the Union by the secession of one or more of the Southern States." In this document, sent to the president-elect Lincoln also, Scott states his fear that if the Union is broken, an effort to restore it by military force would create a state of anarchy in the nation. As a lesser evil he suggested the formation of four new unions, the Eastern Northern States, the Old South, the Middle West, and the Far West. That so distinguished a man as Scott should have made this curious and preposterous suggestion shows how much men's confidence in the perpetuity of the Union had been shaken.

Before Lincoln came to Washington, Scott had entered into correspondence with him, telling him of his wish to co-operate with him in the effort to save the Union. In response to some complimentary words from the president-elect, Scott wrote, using the third person style to which Grant refers, "Lieutenant-General Scott is highly gratified with the favorable opinion entertained of him by the president-elect, as he learns through Senators Baker and Cameron, also personal friends of General Scott, who is happy to reciprocate his highest respect and esteem. The president-elect may rely with confidence on General Scott's utmost exertions in the service of his country (the Union) both before and after the approaching inauguration." To this Lincoln replied, "Permit me to renew to you the assurance of my high appreciation of the many past services you have rendered the Union, and my deep gratification at this evidence of your present active exertions to maintain the integrity and the honor of the nation."

As the day for inauguration approached General Scott was greatly concerned for the safety of Lin-

[17]

coln. He warned him at Philadelphia of the plot to assassinate him, and it was on the strength of this warning that the change of plans was made and the president-elect hurried to Washington secretly and by night. On the day of the inauguration Scott had troops posted throughout the city, and was himself not far from a battery of guns placed in a commanding position. The day previous he had written to Governor Seward a letter dealing with the possible courses to be taken by the new President. He suggested four: 1. Adopt the conciliatory measure of the Crittenden Compromise. 2. Collect duties outside the ports of seceding states, or blockade them. 3. Conquer the seceding states by invading armies. 4. Say to the seceded states, "Wayward sisters, go in peace." General Longstreet in his book, *Manassas to Appomattox,* says that if that policy had been followed and the "wayward sisters" permitted to go out in peace, it would have been but a short time before they would have come back into a stronger Union. But He who decrees the destinies of men and nations had determined otherwise, for not only was the Union to be preserved and restored, but the whole nation was to drink a cup of woe due to those by whom the offense of slavery had come.

General Scott's great wish to avoid a conflict in arms was due to the fact that he was one of the few men who foresaw the desolation and suffering such a war would bring in its train. In commenting on his third possible course for Lincoln to follow, that is, conquer the seceding states by invading armies, he said, "No doubt this might be done in two or

WINFIELD SCOTT

three years, by a young and able general—a Wolfe,
a Dessaix, or a Hoche—with three hundred thousand disciplined men (kept up to that number),
estimating a third for garrisons, and the loss of a
yet greater number by skirmishes, sieges, battles
and Southern fevers. The destruction of life and
property in the other side would be frightful, however perfect the moral discipline of the invaders.
The conquest completed at enormous waste of life
to the North and the Northwest, with at least two
hundred and fifty million dollars added thereto,
and *cui bono?* Fifteen desolated Provinces! Not to
be brought into harmony with their conquerors, to
be held for generations by heavy garrisons, at an
expense quadruple the net duties or taxes which it
would be possible to extort from them, followed by
a Protector or Emperor." However far the venerable general was from understanding the temper
of the North, his certainly was a true and, among
his contemporaries, a rare understanding of what
civil war would mean.

Lincoln had not been in office long before he
directed General Scott to send him a daily report
of the military situation. Thus did the new pilot
of the ship of state at the very beginning put himself into the closest relationship with the direction
of the military efforts of the nation. Colonel A. K.
McClure in his *Lincoln and Men of War Times* relates
a meeting which he and Governor Curtin of Pennsylvania had with Scott and Lincoln at the White
House, a few days after the firing on the flag at
Sumter. McClure and Curtin found Scott waiting
for them in the reception room. The punctilious

old general who could stand only with great discomfort, refused to be seated because there were only two chairs in the room, and remained standing during the wait of half an hour. McClure asked Scott if the capital was not in danger. "No, sir," answered Scott. "No, sir; the capital is not in danger." McClure then, with some hesitation, for he had shared in the reverence with which the public regarded Scott, asked him how many men he had in Washington for its defense. Scott replied, "Fifteen hundred, sir; fifteen hundred men and two batteries." McClure ventured yet further and asked if Washington was a defensible city. With a shadow on his face, Scott answered, "No, sir, Washington is not a defensible city." He then pointed to a sloop of war which was visible in the distant Potomac and said, "You see that vessel?— a sloop of war, sir, a sloop of war." McClure reflected how a battery on the heights of Arlington would make short work of the sloop of war and was not reassured. He then asked the old warrior how many men Beauregard had under him at Charleston. In tremulous tones Scott replied, "General Beauregard commands more men at Charleston than I now command on the continent east of the frontier." McClure then repeated his question, "General, is not Washington in danger?" This roused Scott, who said with soldierly dignity and finality, "No, sir, the capital can't be taken; the capital can't be taken, sir." During the dialogue between McClure and Scott, Lincoln remained a quiet listener, twirling his spectacles around his fingers. When Scott gave his final answer, Lin-

coln said to him, "It does seem to me, General, that
if I were Beauregard I could take Washington."
But this only brought from Scott, with renewed
emphasis, his former assertion, "Mr. President,
the capital can't be taken, sir; it can't be taken."
McClure and Curtin went away from the interview
convinced that the "great Chieftain of two wars
and the worshipped Captain of the Age was in his
dotage and utterly unequal to the great duty of
meeting the impending conflict."

However unfit he may have been for military
execution and leadership, and none is disposed to
doubt that he was, Scott grasped the problems of
the war and comprehended the gigantic task that
was before the nation. He was opposed to a direct
attack through Virginia and proposed instead the
blockade of the ports of the South, while a large
and well-drilled army advanced down the Mississippi Valley to New Orleans. This plan was outlined in a letter Scott wrote to McClellan, in which
he said the Government proposed to raise twenty-
five thousand more regular troops and sixty thousand volunteers for three years. After the autumnal
frosts had killed the virus of malignant fevers in
the river bottoms the invading army of eighty
thousand men, moving partly on the rivers and
partly by land, was to proceed down the Mississippi and clear the Mississippi Valley to the Gulf.
But the populace at the North could not tolerate
the thought of waiting until November before
marching against the enemy, and heaped derision
upon Scott's soldierly plan. The newspapers published cartoons showing a monster serpent, with

General Scott's head, coiled round the Cotton States, and called it "Scott's Anaconda." But wisdom was justified of her children. The ports of the South had to be blockaded and a much larger army than even Scott had proposed had to fight its way to the Gulf, ere the Father of Waters "flowed unvexed to the sea."

General Scott was a Virginian, and when that state seceded from the Union to whose glory it had made so notable a contribution, there were hopes in the South that Scott would do as Lee and other Virginians had done and throw in his lot with the Confederacy. Had not Virginia presented Scott with a handsomely engraved gold sword after his victories in the War of 1812? But they reckoned not with their man. Stephen A. Douglas, on his way to the West to arouse loyalty to the Government, answered the questions about the loyalty of Scott by relating a conversation he had with the Chairman of the Committee of the Virginia Convention appointed to wait on Scott and offer him the command of the Virginia troops. Scott heard them patiently and then said, "I have served my country under the flag of the Union for more than fifty years, and as long as God permits me to live I will defend that flag with my sword, even if my own native state assails it." When the spokesman of the Committee had intimated something about the honor and prestige which might be his if he led the troops of Virginia, Scott held up his hand in solemn protest and said, "Friend Robertson, go no farther. It is best that we part here before you compel me to resent a mortal insult."

Other Virginians who put their country above their state were Admiral Farragut and General Thomas. Robert E. Lee had been Scott's Chief of Staff in Mexico and Scott entertained the highest opinion of his ability. In his memorial address for Lee, at Louisville, General Preston said that long before the Civil War Scott had said to him that Lee was America's greatest living soldier, and added, "I tell you that if I were on my deathbed tomorrow, and the President of the United States should tell me that a great battle was to be fought for the liberty or slavery of the country, and he asked my judgment as to the ability of a commander, I would say with my dying breath, "Let it be Robert E. Lee." When the Civil War came, Scott had not changed his opinion of Lee, and it must have been he who suggested to Lincoln that Lee be asked to take command in the field. Three days after Virginia had seceded, Lincoln sent F. B. Blair, senior, to ask Lee his intentions and unofficially offer him the command of the Union army. Lee declined the offer, saying that although opposed to secession and deprecating war, he could take no part in an invasion of the Southern States. Without a doubt one of the reasons why Lincoln regarded Scott with such admiration and affection was his steadfast loyalty to the Union.

With scores of officers in the army and navy surrendering their commissions and going over to the side of the South every day, Lincoln must have had deep anxiety concerning the loyalty of the remaining officers. The resignation of no officer caused him such pain and amazement as that of Colonel John B. Magruder, 1st Artillery, in command of a light battery on which Scott placed particular reliance for the safety of Washington. When he heard of this officer's defection Lincoln exclaimed, "Only three days ago Magruder came voluntarily to me in this room, and with his own lips and in my presence repeated over and over again his asseveration and protestations of loyalty and fidelity." Scott, at least, Lincoln knew he could trust. Beneath his boasting and pomposity there lay a real veneration for the Constitution and a love for the flag he had served for more than fifty years. Even if his contribution to the military efforts of the country in the crisis of the war was small, the old warrior's patriotic example was worth many regiments of soldiers to the North.

With the impatient and outraged North clamoring for action, and the New York *Tribune* printing every day at the head of its columns the words, "On to Richmond! The rebel Congress must not be allowed to meet there on the 20th of July; by that date the place must be held by the National army!" Lincoln and his political advisers finally decided upon a forward movement of the army which had been assembled about Washington. The fateful council was held at the White House on the 29th of June, with the Cabinet and the chief military officers in attendance. General Scott opposed the move against the Confederate army at Manassas, and favored longer preparation and then a move down the Mississippi Valley. But when his advice was overruled he read to the council a plan of action against Manassas which General McDowell had prepared and which Scott had approved. Scott has been criticized for dividing his forces, one army under McDowell and the other under Patterson near Harper's Ferry. But he was confident that Patterson could keep watch on the force under Joseph E. Johnston opposing him, and should Johnston try to go to reinforce Beauregard at Bull Run, follow hard on his heels. In all this Patterson failed dismally, and McDowell's plans at Bull Run went for nothing because Johnston's army reinforced Beauregard at the critical moment. All through the hours of that eventful Sabbath, Scott was confident of victory, for, as in his Mexican campaigns, he had not let the army go forward until the whole movement had been thoroughly worked out. In the afternoon, when the President came to his office and awakened him out of his sleep, asking for news, Scott reassured him and went off to sleep again!

When the full story of the disaster at the bridge of Bull Run was known, Scott reproached himself for having permitted the army to undertake a campaign which had been against his best judgment. In conversation with the President and the Secretary of War, Scott lost control of himself and exclaimed to the President, "Sir, I am the greatest coward in America. I will prove it. I have fought this battle, sir, against my judgment; I think the President of the United States ought to remove me for doing it. As God is my judge, after my superiors had determined to fight it, I did all in my power to make the army efficient. I deserve removal because I did not stand up when my army was not in condition for fighting and resist it to the last." To this Lincoln answered, "Your conversation seems to imply that I forced you to fight this battle?" General Scott then replied, "I have never served a President who has been kinder to me than you have been."

After this interview it must have been plain to the President that Scott's usefulness as the commander-in-chief was at an end. For some months after McClellan came to take command of the army in the field Scott was retained in supreme command. But McClellan paid him little deference, and reported to the Secretary of War and the President over Scott's head. At length Scott, accepting the inevitable, removed himself from this impossible position by requesting that he be relieved of his command, pleading old age and infirmity. In the order announcing the retirement of Scott, Lincoln said, "The American people will hear with sadness and deep emotion that General Scott has withdrawn from active control of the army, while the President and a unanimous Cabinet express their own and the nation's sympathy in his personal affliction, and their profound sense of the important public services rendered by him to his country during his long and brilliant career, among which will ever be gratefully distinguished his faithful devotion to the Constitution, the Union and the flag when assailed by parricidal rebellion." In his message to Congress, on December 3, 1861, Lincoln called the attention of Congress to the retire-

LINCOLN AND SCOTT

ment of Scott in these words, "Since your last adjournment Lieutenant-General Scott has retired from the head of the army. During his long life the nation has not been unmindful of his merit; yet, on calling to mind how faithfully, ably and brilliantly he has served the country, from a time far back in our history when few of the now living had been born, and thenceforward continually, I cannot but think we are still his debtors. I submit, therefore, for your consideration what further mark of recognition is due to him and to ourselves as a grateful people." In 1863, General Scott, who hitherto had been only a Brevet Lieutenant-General was made a full Lieutenant-General.

General McClellan relates how at four o'clock on a dark November morning he saw his former chief off on the train when he left Washington. In a philosophical turn of mind he thus meditates on the exit of Scott: "The sight of this morning was a lesson to me which I hope not soon to forget. I saw there the end of a long, active and ambitious life, the end of the career of the first soldier of his nation; and it was a feeble old man, scarce able to walk, hardly any one there to see him off but his successor. Should I ever become vainglorious and ambitious, remind me of that spectacle." In less than a year General McClellan, stripped of his high command, departed from the same station and made way for his successors. So passes the glory of this world.

Only twice again did Lincoln and Scott meet in this world. The first meeting was at West Point in the latter part of June, 1862. The only record of this mysterious meeting is a memorandum from the hand of Scott for the President, giving his advice on the military situation and urging that General McDowell's division which was being held back from McClellan be sent forward at once. This letter was written just two days before Lee attacked McClellan's right at Cold Harbor and began the Seven Days' battle. It is significant that at so critical a juncture Lincoln should have absented himself from the capital and gone to West Point to consult with the retired Lieutenant-General. There could be no better evidence of how highly Lincoln esteemed his counsel. It is generally supposed that at this meeting General Scott advised Lincoln to call Halleck to Washington as Commander-in-Chief and unite the three independent armies of Fremont, Banks and McDowell under General Pope. This was the course soon followed by Lincoln. The second and last meeting between Scott and Lincoln was when the latter lay in state at the City Hall in New York, and the venerable Lieutenant-General was the most conspicuous among the thousands of mourners who passed by the still form of the martyred President, whose military and political perplexities were now forever at an end.

LINCOLN AND FREMONT

When the Civil War broke out there was no man to whom, as an organizer of victory, the people of the North looked with greater hope and confidence than they did to John C. Fremont. He was in France when hostilities commenced, but returned at once. The leaders of the Government regarded him with the same favor in which he was held by the people at large. As early as December, 1860, Seward had suggested him to Lincoln for Secretary of War, and upon his return from Europe, July 1, 1861, when he landed at New York he was handed his commission as major-general in the regular army, and three days later was assigned to the Department of Missouri, with headquarters at St. Louis. Meade was not made a major-general in the regular army until after Gettysburg, and Thomas not until after Nashville; but Fremont, as soon as he appeared on the shores of his native land was given this high rank and appointed to one of the most important commands in the whole field of military operations. But not many months were to pass by before the people and the Government suffered a great disappointment and disillusionment as to the capacities of their hero. No man in the Union Army rose so quickly to so high an eminence; none suffered so complete an eclipse of fame.

It will be clear to the reader that the man who was given so high a rank and so important a post by his Government, and with the unanimous approval of the people of the country, must have possessed a more than ordinary personality. What was it about Fremont that had captured the public admiration and won the esteem of the thoughtful men who were anxiously casting about for captains who should lead the armies to victory and put down the rebellion? The best answer to this is a brief sketch of Fremont.

John C. Fremont was born in Savanah, Georgia, in 1813, the son of a French father and a Virginian mother. As a student at the College of Charleston he showed marked ability in the field of mathematics, but his disregard of discipline led to his expulsion from the college. Some years later he was appointed an instructor of mathematics on board the sloop of war *Natchez*, and after his return from a long cruise to South America was appointed a professor in the United States Navy. But he chose instead to take employment in companies surveying routes for railroads over the mountains from Charleston to Cincinnati. In 1838 he was commissioned Second Lieutenant of Topographical Engineers in the United States Army, and served for three years as an assistant to Nicollet, the French surveyor, who had been engaged by the Government to survey the territory lying between the upper waters of the Mississippi and the Missouri Rivers. The young engineer had strengthened his position by marrying Jessie Benton, the gifted and beautiful daughter of the famous senator from Missouri, Thomas H. Benton. Through the influence of Benton, Fremont secured successive

JOHN C. FREMONT

commissions to explore and survey the whole Rocky Mountain territory. His official reports of the experiences of his party, the lakes, mountains, rivers, thrilling escapes in rushing torrents or from encounters with wild beasts or wilder savages, were read with the greatest avidity by the people, and Fremont's name was upon every lip. At the time of the outbreak of the Mexican War, Fremont, then on the Pacific Coast, helped to complete the conquest of California. His activities brought him into conflict with the military commander, General Philip Kearny, afterwards killed at the second battle of Bull Run, and Fremont was sent to Washington under arrest. There a court-martial found him guilty of mutiny, disobedience and conduct prejudicial to military discipline, and sentenced him to be dismissed from the service. President Polk approved the findings of the court-martial, except as to mutiny. This trial did no injury whatever to Fremont's growing reputation. He continued under private auspices his explorations and surveys in the West, and in 1849 was elected as one of the first senators from California.

At the Convention of the National Republican party in Philadelphia in 1856 Fremont was unanimously and enthusiastically elected as the first standard bearer of the Republican party, his youth, good looks, superior education, the thrill and romance of his exploits in the great West and his denunciations of slavery, all combining to make him an ideal candidate fitted to kindle the enthusiasms of the young voters and lead to victory the newborn party. In the exciting and feverish campaign which followed, Fremont was defeated by Buchanan. Yet his popular vote was not far behind that of the successful candidate. One of the incidents of the campaign was the charge that Fremont was a Catholic, it being the time when there was a party in the field with an anti-Catholic plank in its platform. One of the chief things brought forward as evidence that Fremont was a Catholic was the fact that he had carved the Cross on the side of one of the mountains he had discovered in the far West, thus following in the path of De Soto and Columbus and other Roman Catholic discoverers.

Although defeated for the Presidency, Fremont's fame was secure, and when the Civil War began it was inevitable that he should be regarded as one of the men, if not the man, for the hour. It will be observed that the career of Fremont, from his youthful escapades down to his leading the Republican party in its first battle, had in it all those elements which arouse the interest of the people and invest personality with a halo of romance and popular interest. When the great day came which was to try men's souls, everybody looked for great things from Fremont, the "Pathfinder." As he had found a path to the Pacific through the wilderness of the West, so now, it was confidently held, he would show the way for the subjugation of the South and the salvation of the Union.

For his chief political backing, if indeed, with his popularity in the nation, he required such backing, Fremont had the support of the remarkable Blair family of Missouri. The senior Blair, Francis P., had been for many years editor of the *Globe* at St. Louis. One son, Montgomery, was the Postmaster-General, and Francis P., Jr., the ablest of the three, had long been prominent in Democratic politics. His energy and loyalty played a great part in saving Missouri for the Union. Two years after the resignation of Fremont from the service Lincoln said that it was at the earnest solicitation of the Blairs that he was made a general and sent to St. Louis. But before Fremont had finished his chapter in the military history of the war, the Blairs, who had brought him forward, became his bitter enemies.

Fremont received his commission as major-general in the Regular Army on July 1, 1861, and had the Western Department, comprising the territory of Missouri, Illinois, Kentucky and Kansas, created for him on July 3rd. But two weeks passed before he accepted his commission and almost a month before he appeared at St. Louis, and that in spite of the critical state of affairs in that sector. Montgomery Blair, the Postmaster-General, relates how embarrassed he was during this period of delay by the President's daily inquiries as to the movements of Fremont. The creation of a new army is always a difficult undertaking, and Fremont soon showed his complete ineptitude for his task. Honest himself, he became the prey of contractors and rogues who exploited his department for their own profit. General Sherman tells how, on a visit to Fremont's headquarters, he was surprised to find there in places of trust and influence so many of the rogues and knaves he had known when in California, and says that when he saw them there came to his mind the saying, "Where the vultures are, there is a carcass close by." And such indeed proved to be the case.

Fremont's utter lack of ability to organize an army and plan for victory was accompanied by extreme military pomp and parade. He had for his bodyguard a band of horsemen some of whom were Hungarians, among them the gallant Major Zagonyi. Of all high commanders Fremont was the most difficult of access, and that very isolation and inaccessibility was one of the causes of his downfall. On August 10, 1861, the heroic General Lyon was killed while leading a charge against the immensely superior Confederate force at Wilson's Creek, and the army he had commanded retreated northward. This reverse, due to the dilatoriness of Fremont in sending up reinforcements, made Fremont, heretofore accustomed only to popular favor, the object of severe criticism. He now began to bestir himself, but his activities seemed to arouse everywhere complaint and suspicion, and it was openly hinted that he had some secret purpose of trying Aaron Burr's scheme of setting up a dictatorship in the southwest.

When these complaints about Fremont began to come through to Washington, Lincoln sent by the hand of the Postmaster-General a letter to General David Hunter, one of the division commanders of Fremont, requesting Hunter to use his influence and ability in helping and advising Fremont. This letter, which shows how kind and considerate Lincoln was in dealing with men whom he had appointed to high office and who were not fulfilling his expectations, ran as follows:

My dear Sir:

General Fremont needs assistance which it is diffi-cult to give him. He is losing the confidence of men near him, whose support any man in his position must have to be successful. His cardinal mistake is that he isolates himself, and allows nobody to see him; and by which he does not know what is going on in the very matter he is dealing with. He needs to have by his side a man of large experience. Will you not, for me, take that place? Your rank is one grade too high to be ordered to it; but will you not serve the country and oblige me by taking it voluntarily?

In the meantime there had come an open rupture between Colonel Francis P. Blair and Fremont, Blair preferring charges against Fremont for mal-administration, and Fremont placing Blair under arrest. On his way to Fremont, Montgomery Blair passed Mrs. Fremont on her way to Washington as an indignant and zealous advocate of her hus-band's cause and fortune. She sought an inter-view with Lincoln at midnight, asked for copies of the confidential letters about her husband's case and intimated that if General Fremont should de-cide to try conclusions with Lincoln, he could set up for himself without difficulty. In speaking of this interview Lincoln said, "She taxed me so violently with many things that I had to exercise all the awkward tact I have to avoid quarreling with her."

In the newspapers of August 30, 1861, Lincoln read the report of a proclamation which had just been issued by Fremont in his department. In this startling proclamation Fremont declared martial law throughout the State of Missouri and further ordered that all persons taken with arms in their hands within his lines should be tried by court-martial and, if found guilty, shot. He further declared that the property of all persons in arms against the United States was confiscated to the public use, and their slaves, if they possessed them, were freemen. It has generally been supposed that Fremont had been stung by the criticism which had been directed towards him since the Union reverse at Wilson's Creek, and that he hit upon this method of restoring himself to public favor.

As soon as he had an authentic copy of the despatch, Lincoln wrote to Fremont remonstrating with him and asking him to modify the confiscation and slave clause so as to conform to the act of Congress. In this letter the President said:

My dear Sir:
Two points in your proclamation of August 30 give me some anxiety:
First.—Should you shoot a man, according to the proclamation, the Confederates would very certainly shoot our best men in their hands in retaliation; and so, man for man, indefinitely. It is, therefore, my order that you allow no man to be shot under the proclamation without first having my approbation or consent.
Second.—I think there is great danger that the closing paragraph, in relation to the confiscation of property and the liberating slaves of traitorous owners, will alarm our Southern Union friends and turn them against us, perhaps ruin our rather fair prospect for Kentucky. Allow me, therefore, to ask that you will,

as of your own notion, modify that paragraph so as
to conform to the first and fourth sections of the act
of Congress entitled "An Act to confiscate property
used for insurrectionary purposes," approved August
6, 1861, and a copy of such act I herewith send you.
  This letter is written in a spirit of caution, and not
of censure. I send it by my special messenger, in
order that it may certainly and speedily reach you.

In answer to the President's letter Fremont
wrote that the proclamation had been the inspira-
tion of a single night, and that it was designed to
meet the dangers which he foresaw in the situation which confronted him, the combination of the
rebel armies, the Provisional Government and
home traitors. He declared that he could not of
his own volition withdraw or modify the proclamation, for that would imply that he had changed his
mind as to its necessity and wisdom, which he had
not; but he would so modify it in obedience to an
order from the President. This order was forthcoming at once and the proclamation modified as
the President had directed. As for the shooting
clause, Fremont correctly stated that what he
meant was the shooting of civilians who took up
arms against an army of occupation and that he
had no thought of shooting prisoners of war. One
of the Confederate commanders in Missouri issued
a counter-proclamation, as the President had an-
ticipated, declaring that for every soldier of the
state guard or Southern army so put to death he
would "hang, draw and quarter a minion of Abraham Lincoln's." How much of this was pure
bluff, only the rigid enforcement of Fremont's
proclamation could have determined. But the

careful student of the first months of the war will be impressed with the fact that while Fremont's policy of dealing with the insurrectionary population was perhaps too severe, as he outlined it in his proclamation, that pursued by Lincoln was far too mild and conciliatory. A little more severity in those first months, teaching the people that it was not a summer picnic to rebel against the Government of the United States, might have saved the life of many a soldier, North and South.

Lincoln's chief objection to Fremont's proclamation, however, was to the clause about emancipating the slaves of persons in arms against the Government. This attitude of not molesting the slaves was the policy of the Chicago platform on which Lincoln stood when elected, and a principle he had carefully enunciated. The grim logic of military and political history was soon to compel him to depart from that policy. But the hour was not yet come. He was particularly solicitous about the border states and the effect Fremont's proclamation would have upon them, especially upon Kentucky, then in the balance. In a letter to the Honorable O. H. Browning on this subject, Lincoln cites the case of a company of Union volunteers from Kentucky who threw down their arms and went home when they heard of Fremont's emancipation proclamation. Moreover, he regarded Fremont's action as a piece of usurpation of civil authority on the part of the military authority. Here again the verdict of history will be that Lincoln overestimated the damage that might have been done by Fremont's proclamation and underestimated its good effects. In a little more than a year Lincoln himself, after the battle of Antietam, issued a preliminary proclamation of emancipation as a military measure, precisely on the grounds of Fremont's. But by that time the suffering of the war, the perils of the government, and the sweep of sentiment in the North, with the effect such a proclamation would have upon foreign governments, particularly upon the British Government, making it impossible that England should intervene in the war as against the side which had set out to destroy slavery—all these made emancipation natural if not inevitable. Undoubtedly, if a proclamation of emancipation was to be made it should have been universal and by the government, and not by any one commander in the field. In this Lincoln was right. But that such a proclamation issued in the summer of 1861 would have seriously damaged the Union cause, or would have failed to meet with support in the North, cannot now be seriously entertained. As it was, the proclamation of Fremont aroused the greatest enthusiasm in the North. Herndon, Lincoln's law partner, said, "Fremont's proclamation was right; Lincoln's modification of it was wrong." Senator Grimes of Iowa said, "The people are all with Fremont and will uphold him through thick and thin—every body of every sect, party, sex, and color approves his proclamation in the Southwest and it will not do for the administration to causelessly tamper with the man who had the sublime moral courage to issue it." Henry Ward Beecher said in his pulpit, "I cannot but express my conviction that both our government, and in some greater degree the community, have done great injustice to the cause in Missouri, in the treatment it has bestowed upon that noble man, General Fremont."

After the disaster which befell Colonel Mulligan's force at Lexington, on the Missouri River, a disaster attributed to the dilatoriness and incompetence of Fremont, Lincoln grew anxious and dispatched the Secretary of War, Cameron, accompanied by the Adjutant-General of the Army, to Fremont's headquarters. In a letter to the President, Cameron tells how he interviewed Fremont and of the latter's grief and mortification when Cameron showed him an order for his removal. In response to his urgent appeal Cameron promised to withhold the order until he had returned to Washington, thus giving Fremont time to take some decisive action, with the understanding that if he should be successful he would not be removed, but if he remained inactive or failed, another officer would take his place. Cameron asked General Hunter point blank if he thought Fremont fit for his command and Hunter replied that he did not. Another officer, General Samuel R. Curtis, in answer to the President's questions, declared that Fremont lacked the "intelligence, experience and sagacity" necessary to such a command, and that his removal was only a question of manner and time. Public opinion is an element of war which must not be neglected. None knew this better than Lincoln, and without question, public opinion played its part in holding back the hand of Lincoln when it ought to have removed Fremont from the command for which he was obviously unfitted.

LINCOLN AND FREMONT

At length the long-delayed order for the removal came to Fremont through Curtis. But the letter of Lincoln to Curtis again shows his wonderful patience and kindness and too great reluctance to wound an officer's feelings, even when the good of the cause was involved. In this letter to Curtis Lincoln said:

Dear Sir:
On receipt of this with the accompanying enclosures, you will take safe, certain and suitable measures to have the enclosure addressed to Major-General Fremont delivered to him with all reasonable dispatch, subject to these conditions only, that if, when General Fremont shall be reached by the messenger—yourself or any one sent by you—he shall then have in personal command, fought and won a battle, or shall be in the immediate presence of the enemy in expectation of a battle, it is not to be delivered, but held for further orders. After, and not until after the delivery to General Fremont, let the enclosure addressed to General Hunter be delivered to him."

The agent of Curtis found Fremont far from any engagement, and the President's orders were carried out and he was superseded by Hunter. The remark in Lincoln's letter to Curtis about taking "safe, certain and suitable measures" to deliver to Fremont the order for his removal reveals a degree of anxiety in the President's mind as to the possible effect of this order upon the supporters and defenders of Fremont, for through his ante-bellum record and his personal charm Fremont was still most popular with his army and the people of Missouri. But like a true soldier Fremont obeyed the order for his removal with promptness and dignity and the change was effected with hardly a ripple of excitement. When Fremont returned to St. Louis the people gave him a remarkable demonstration and presented him with a gold sword. It was more like the return of a victorious marshal than the retirement of an unsuccessful general.

Fremont was not long out of employment, for Lincoln created for him the Department of the Mountains, embracing the West Virginia mountains and adjacent territory. His appointment was due to the great kindness of the President, who wished to give him another chance, and also to the fact that he was still a popular figure with thousands of people in the North who considered that he had been ill-used in Missouri. In May, 1862, when McClellan was operating against Richmond, "Stonewall" Jackson broke out in the Shenandoah Valley, defeating Banks at Winchester and compelling him to retreat upon the Potomac. It was at this juncture that Lincoln detached McDowell's corps from McClellan's army and sent it to aid in the pursuit of Jackson. Shields, of McDowell's army, was to go into the Shenandoah Valley from the east, Fremont from the mountains in the west, and Banks from the north. It was a bit of strategy worked out by Lincoln and it ought to have succeeded, for Jackson was between three armies. That it did not succeed was due in part to the slowness of Fremont, who permitted Jackson to reach Strassburg before he did, although Jackson had been marching and fighting for a month. Had

LINCOLN AND FREMONT

Fremont followed the route telegraphed him by Lincoln he would have intercepted Jackson, but he chose another route and the result was the escape of the Confederate army. After this fiasco the three armies, Fremont's, Banks', and McDowell's, were united as the Army of Virginia with General Pope commanding. Fremont considered it an affront to his dignity to serve under Pope, whom he outranked, and resigned his commission. With much better reason the other two commanders, Banks and McDowell, might have resented being put under Pope, but like true soldiers and patriots they acquiesced in the new arrangement. This closing incident of Fremont's military career was the least creditable to him and gives us an index to his character. In him the ego was supreme, not in the offensive manner of some, for those who came into personal contact with him were always charmed; but his quitting the service of the country at one of the darkest hours of the Civil War reveals the fact that he put self above country. His conduct in asking to be relieved when Pope was appointed over him is comparable to that of another military egoist, General Hooker, who left Sherman's army in Georgia when Sherman chose Howard to succeed the fallen McPherson.

In the spring of 1863 Lincoln was importuned to create a new department for General Fremont, putting him at the head of all the colored troops. Lincoln, in spite of his past experiences with Fremont, took the matter under consideration. Fortunately for the country the appointment was not made. The singular hold that Fremont had on the imagination of the people is revealed by the fact that when in 1863 the administration was looking about for a new commander for the Army of the Potomac to take the place of Hooker, one faction in the Cabinet was urging the appointment of Fremont. With Fremont in command at Gettysburg instead of Meade, it is not hard to imagine what would have happened.

General Sherman relates that when he rode on the train with Grant from Chattanooga to Cincinnati, after Grant had been made commander of all the armies, one of the topics Grant discussed with him was the possibility of getting back into the service high officers who had retired from active command. Among those mentioned were Buell, McClellan, Crittenden, McCook and Fremont.

In the summer of 1864 Fremont was nominated as the candidate for President by the convention of radical Republicans meeting in Cleveland. In this convention were many malcontents, and men who had fallen out with the administration. When he was reading the reports coming in from the Cleveland convention and was told that instead of the thousands who were expected to be present, the convention numbered only four hundred, the President reached for the Bible which lay on his desk and, turning to the passage in Samuel I, read, "And everyone that was in distress, and everyone that was in debt, and everyone that was discontented, gathered themselves unto him; and he became a captain over them; and there were with him about four hundred men." This was the best possible comment on the Cleveland convention. After a few denunciations of Lincoln and his policies, Fremont saw the drift of events and during the summer withdrew from the race. Thus his political campaign, like his military campaigns, ended in a fiasco.

LINCOLN AND BUTLER

Many years ago there could be seen standing in front of one of the newspaper offices in New York a miniature statue of a man with a spoon over his shoulder. The statue was that of Benjamin F. Butler and had been placed there by one of his numerous haters. The spoon was supposed to remind the passerby of Butler's alleged graft and spoliation when in command at New Orleans. Probably no man in our national life has been so fiercely hated and bitterly denounced as General Butler. Even so sober and restrained a man as the late Senator George F. Hoar in his *Sketch of Seventy Years* gives expression to what is almost a righteous horror of the character of his dead antagonist. He says of him:

"No person can adequately comprehend the political history of Massachusetts for the thirty-five years beginning with 1850 without a knowledge of the character, career and behaviour of Benjamin F. Butler. It is, of course, disagreeable and in most cases unmanly to speak harshly of a political antagonist who is dead. In the presence of the great reconciler, Death, ordinary human contentions and angers should be hushed. But if there be such a thing in the universe as a moral law, if the distinction between right and wrong be other than fancy or a dream, the difference between General Butler and the men who contended with him belongs not to this life alone. It relates to matters more permanent than human life. It enters into the fate of republics, and will endure after the fashion of this world passeth away."

BENJAMIN F. BUTLER

LINCOLN AND BUTLER

From this solemn and prophet-like indictment by the grave Senator from Massachusetts, clear down to the hoarse screams of the canaille of the streets of New Orleans, there rises against "Butler the Beast," as Beauregard called him, a most extraordinary chorus of hatred and denunciation. Butler was one of those men born to draw the fire of their fellowmen. Born at Deerfield and educated at the Baptist College at Waterville, Maine, now Colby, Butler established himself as a lawyer at Lowell, Massachusetts, where his ready repartee and rough invective made him feared by other lawyers. He espoused the cause of the operatives in the factories who were striving to secure a ten-hour law, and when some of the factories posted a notice warning their employes that all those who voted for the ticket advocating such a measure would be discharged, Butler defied them. In characteristic language he said that if a single workman were discharged he would lead them in reducing Lowell to a sheep pasture and a fishing place, and would commence by applying the torch to his own house.

In 1860 Butler was delegate to the Democratic National Convention which met at Charleston, South Carolina. He had been instructed to vote for Douglas, but distinguished himself by voting for Jefferson Davis fifty-seven times. As soon as armed secession became imminent Butler let all men know where he stood. In conversation with members of the National Committee of the Breckenridge wing of the Democratic party, who told him of the plan to secede and who said that Massachusetts would not be able to resist secession because such a policy would be opposed by thousands of her own citizens, Butler answered:

"No, sir; when we come from Massachusetts on this errand, we shall not leave a single traitor behind, unless he is hanging on a tree."

"Well, we shall see."

"You will see. I know something of the North and a good deal about New England, where I was born and have lived for forty-two years. We are pretty quiet there now because we don't believe you mean to carry out your threat. We have heard the same story at every election these twenty years. Our people don't believe you are in earnest. But let me tell you, as sure as you attempt to destroy this Union, the North will resist the attempt to its last man and its last dollar. One thing you may do, you may ruin the Southern States, and extinguish your institution of slavery. From the moment your first gun is fired on the American flag your slaves will not be worth five years' purchase. But as to breaking up the Union, it cannot be done. God and nature, and the blood of your fathers and mine have made it one, and one country it must and shall remain."

Afterwards, in conversation with the South Carolina Commissioners, who were in Washington to present the ordinance of secession to the President, a similar conversation occurred. They said to him:

"The North won't fight."

"The North will fight."

"If the North fights, its laborers will starve and overturn the government."

"If the South fights, there is an end of slavery."

"Do you mean to say that you, yourself, would fight in such a cause?"

"I would: and by the grace of God, I will!"

It is not strange that the author of such sentiments should have been one of the first to march to the defense of the Government when the flag was fired on at Sumter. His brigade of Massachusetts militia was the first to get to Washington, one of the regiments, the Sixth, being attacked in the streets of Baltimore. Butler followed with the other regiments of his brigade, and by vigorous measures reopened communications with Washington by way of Havre de Grace and Annapolis. Made ranking major-general of volunteers for his vigorous and patriotic actions, Butler commanded the Federal troops in the fiasco at Big Bethel. His elevation to so high a rank was due in part to the great energy he had displayed at the critical time when Lincoln was wondering whether there were any North, and whether the troops would ever arrive for the defense of the capital, and in part to the fact that he was a prominent Democratic politician. As in the case of John McClernand, of Illinois, Lincoln was very careful to give recognition to prominent men in the opposition party who at the beginning of the war took a fearless stand for the Union, and this exerted great influence upon their followers. When he accepted this commission as the ranking major-general of volunteers, Butler said to Lincoln:

"I will accept the commission with many thanks to you for your personal kindness. But there is one thing I must say to you as we don't know each other. That as a Democrat I opposed your election and did all I could for your opponent. But I shall do no political act, and loyally support your administration as long as I hold your commission; and when I find any act that I cannot support I shall bring the commission back at once, and return it to you."

To this Lincoln answered:

"That is frank and fair. But I want to add one thing: When you see me doing anything that for the good of the country ought not to be done, come and tell me so, and why you think so, and then perhaps you won't have any chance to resign your commission."

In accepting the commission Butler had said something about whether or not he ought to forsake his law practice, and how he had left a case he was trying in the courts at Boston. Lincoln looked at him with a whimsical expression and said, "I guess we both wish we were back trying cases!"

Butler was the inventor of the happy phrase "Contraband of War." When in command at Fortress Monroe he refused to return to their owners slaves who had come within the Union lines, on the ground that being useful to their employers who were in arms against the Government they were contraband of war. Three negroes belonging to Colonel Mallory had come within the Union works. The next day a Confederate major came in under a flag of truce and asked in the name of Colonel Mallory for the return of the negroes. When Butler declared his intention to hold them, the major asked him how he could thus set aside the constitutional obligation to return them. Butler responded that he had taken Virginia at her word in the act of secession and that regarding her as a foreign country he was conscious of no constitutional obligation towards her. "But," said the major, "you say we cannot secede, and so you cannot consistently detain the negroes." "But you say you *have* seceded," rejoined Butler with his ever ready repartee, "so you cannot consistently claim them. I shall hold these negroes as contraband of war, since they are engaged in construction of your battery and are claimed as your property. The question is simply whether they shall be used for or against the Government of the United States."

Butler says that as a lawyer he was never very proud of the phrase "contraband of war," but that it was a great help to him in the discharge of his duty and in meeting the difficult problems of runaway slaves. His policy was the one adopted by the armies operating against the Confederacy. Thus a most perplexing problem was solved in a very practical way, for the Union soldiers would never have submitted to the task of acting as a marshal's posse in returning fugitive slaves to their masters.

From the very outset of the war Butler was convinced that the Government exercised too much clemency and leniency in dealing with the revolted states. Most students of the period will agree that this was true, and that if war is to be waged it must be sternly waged. "I have often been asked," wrote Butler, "why our war was so protracted. Was not the pusillanimity and want of executive force of the government as exhibited in this transaction, one sufficient answer? Why was not Pickett hanged for these twenty-two deliberate murders when he was captured by us?" The reference is to the fact that General Pickett hanged twenty-two men of the Second North Carolina Regiment (Federal) on the ground that they had

[51]

formerly been in the ranks of the Confederate army and were therefore deserters.

This exercise of too much leniency was the one matter in which Butler was at odds with his tender-hearted commander-in-chief. In one of his conferences with Lincoln, Butler spoke of the many desertions in the Army of the Potomac and advised punishment by death as the only effectual means of stopping it. To this Lincoln responded with distressed face and tone, "How can I have a butcher's day every Friday in the Army of the Potomac!" "Better have that," answered Butler, "than have the Army of the Potomac so depleted by desertions that good men will be butchered on other days than Friday."

Butler's career at New Orleans was, on the whole, the most creditable in his long service to the Government. Whatever Butler was or was not, no one ever called him a coward. When he took his troops into the turbulent city, he marched at their head in order to give them confidence. From the very beginning his administration was marked with severity and fearlessness, yet with justice and equity. He established his headquarters at the *St. Charles Hotel,* and in the morning sent for the city government. As he was conferring with the mayor and other members of the city government, the mob gathered in the street below and became so boisterous that it was with extreme difficulty the negotiations could be carried on. Finally Captain De Kay, one of General Williams' staff, came in with his uniform almost torn from him, and reported that the mob was getting out of hand. Butler at once responded, "Give my compliments to General Williams and tell him to clear the streets at once with his artillery."

When the captain left with the order the city officials jumped to their feet and entreated Butler not to send such an order. Butler answered that if they could quiet the mob, they were at liberty to try. It made no difference to him how it was done, just so it was done quickly. The mayor and another gentleman then attempted speeches from the balcony, but the mob jeered in their faces. Butler was a little withdrawn from the window when he heard the cry go up, "Where's old Butler? Let him show himself; let him come out here if he dare!" Immediately Butler stepped out onto the balcony in full view of the mob, and with cap in hand said, "Who calls me? I am here!" With that a hush began to steal over the cowed mob. At that moment Butler heard a sound, and looking up St. Charles Street saw the Sixth Maine Battery's six Napoleons come thundering down the roughly paved street, the wheels of the guns bounding high into the air as they struck the stones and ruts. Before the roaring avalanche the mob vanished and the street became as quiet as a children's playground. The mob never troubled Butler again in New Orleans.

From the very beginning of his reign Butler made it plain that there was such a thing as the Government of the United States and that its soldiers and officers could not be insulted with impunity. A private went into a shoe store, and selecting a pair of shoes, offered gold for them. The proprietor declared that he would not sell shoes to a d— Yankee. The next day the provost marshal had a red flag floating over the shop and sold the whole stock at auction.

The filthy condition of the city, especially in the numerous canals and in the back yards of the finer homes, was a menace to the lives of his soldiers and an invitation to the great pest of the place, yellow fever. Butler, using his own common sense, made New Orleans safe and healthy during the months of his stay in the city. It was prophetic of the work of the United States Army in Cuba and the Philippines.

While in New Orleans Butler was served by a marvelously efficient secret service corps, by means of which he kept himself informed as to the inmost councils of the secessionists in the town. As it was in the day of Benhadad and Elisha, the words spoken in the bedchamber were soon repeated to Butler, not through aides or officers, but to him in person. This information came through the negroes. On one occasion Butler learned that a well-to-do woman was having a sewing party every night at her house, and that she had just completed a beautiful gold embroidered Confederate flag for presentation to the army at Corinth. The next morning Butler sent his calash for the lady and had her wait upon him at his office in the Custom House. Butler informed her that he had learned of how she had just completed a handsome flag. His own home town, Lowell, Massachusetts, he said, was soon to have a celebration for the Sabbath-school children, and, as many of them had never seen a Confederate flag, he would like to borrow hers.

During the days of McClellan's unsuccessful campaign in the Peninsula, the most sensational rumors were abroad in New Orleans as to the disaster which had befallen the Union army. Butler tested the truth of the rumors by having his secret service men report whether the Jew brokers were buying or selling Confederate treasury notes. If they were selling them, as was generally the case, he knew that no serious disaster had come upon the Union cause. In those days a German bookseller exhibited a skeleton in his window and labeled it "Chickahominy Yankee," pretending that it was the skeleton of one of McClellan's soldiers. Another individual, a cousin of Massachusetts' war governor, Andrew, appeared at the Louisiana Club with a breast pin constructed (so he claimed) of the thigh bone of a Yankee soldier killed on the Chickahominy. Now the interesting and picturesque thing about General Butler was the way he dealt with these insults and provocations. More cautious men would have let them pass, but be it said to Butler's credit that he never let an insult to the majesty of the United States pass without at least an effort to punish the offender. The man with the stickpin was hailed before the General, who said to him:

"Did you exhibit such a pin?"

"Yes, sir; I was wearing it."

"Did you say it was made of the thigh bone of a Yankee?"

"Yes; but it was not true, General."

"Then you added lying to your other accomplishments in trying to disgrace the army of your country. I will sentence you to hard labor on Ship Island for two years."

The two most famous incidents of his administration at New Orleans were the hanging of Mumford and the "woman order." Mumford, who was at the head of the gambling ring in New Orleans, and had much power with the people, led the mob that tore down the United States flag which Farragut had raised over the Mint. One of the pieces of the torn flag he wore in his buttonhole as an ornament. The first day Butler was in New Orleans he noted this man Mumford in the mob before the hotel wearing the bit of the flag. Inquiring who he was, Butler vowed he would hang him when caught. In due time he was arrested, tried, convicted and sentenced to be hanged. The most extraordinary influence was brought to bear upon Butler for his pardon. It was openly boasted in the city that Butler would not dare to hang the man. Threats poured in on him, warning him that his life would be in forfeit should Mumford be executed. Even notable citizens came to plead for the condemned gambler, saying that his execution would let loose the fury of the populace. As a last resort Mumford's weeping wife and children were sent to Butler's headquarters. But nothing could move him. Imitating the Spanish custom which places the scene of the execution as near as possible to the place of the crime, Butler, with poetic justice, ordered that the man should be hanged at the Mint, where he had torn down the nation's flag. A great throng gathered, shouting that Butler would not dare carry out the execution. Mumford made them an oration declaring that he had been impelled by the highest patriotism. As the appointed hour drew near Mumford looked anxiously up the street for the expected reprieve. But none came. The drop fell and the offense against the nation's flag was expiated. It was a severe measure, but if more severity had been exercised by the Federal Government at the beginning of the war many thousands of lives might have been spared.

After Mumford had been hanged, Jefferson Davis issued a proclamation declaring that Butler was no longer to be treated "simply as a public enemy of the Confederate States of America, but as an outlaw and common enemy of mankind, and in the event of his capture the officer in command of the capturing force shall cause him to be immediately executed by hanging."

The incident which made Butler's name anathema in the South was the general order which he issued for the protection of the United States soldiers from the insults of the women of New Orleans. These insults reached their climax one Sabbath morning when one of Butler's officers with a prayer book in hand was on his way to church. Meeting two well-dressed young women he stepped aside to make way for them, when one of the ladies deliberately stepped in front of him and spat full in his face. The humiliated and disgusted officer asked Butler's permission to resign, saying that he had enlisted to fight the enemies of his country, not to be insulted and humiliated. Butler saw that something must be done. From his legal knowledge he recalled the language of an old English ordinance, and the next day the following order was published in the city:

"As the officers and soldiers of the United States have been subjected to repeated insults from the women (calling themselves ladies) of New Orleans, in return for the most scrupulous non-interference and courtesy on your part, it is ordered that hereafter when any female shall, by word, gesture or movement, insult or show contempt for any officer or soldier of the United States, she shall be regarded and held liable to be treated as a woman of the town plying her avocation."

This order, as the shrewd Butler foresaw, was immediately effective, for ladies would not now insult a soldier for fear they would be regarded as common women, and women of the lower ranks also refrained from their vexatious abuse because they wished to be regarded as ladies. No other incident of the war so enraged the South as this order. Officers of the Confederate army read it to their troops on parade so as to stir up their martial ardor. Palmerston, British premier, affected to be shocked by it, and speaking in the House of Commons said, "An Englishman must blush to think that such an act has been committed by one belonging to the Anglo-Saxon race." To this sneer of the British prime minister Butler made indirect answer in his extraordinary farewell address to the citizens of New Orleans. In this address he said:

LINCOLN AND BUTLER

"To be sure, I might have regaled you with the amenities of British civilization, and yet have been within the supposed rules of civilized warfare. You might have been smoked to death in caverns as were the Covenanters of Scotland by the command of a general of the royal house of England, or roasted like the inhabitants of Algiers during the French campaign; your wives and daughters might have been given over to the ravisher, as were the unfortunate dames of Spain during the Peninsular war; or you might have been scalped and tomahawked, as our mothers were at Wyoming by the savage allies of Great Britain in our own Revolution. Your sons might have been blown from the mouths of cannon, like the Sepoys at Delhi; and yet all this would have been within the rules of civilized warfare as practised by the most polished and most hypocritical nations of Europe."

The indignation aroused by the "woman order" and the protests of foreign governments as to the trade restrictions of Butler's administration, were probably the reasons for his recall. When Butler saw Lincoln after his recall from New Orleans he asked him why he had been recalled. "Oh," said Lincoln, "ask Seward. Something about foreign governments, I guess." Butler, however, continued to enjoy the confidence of Lincoln, who even offered him Grant's command on the Mississippi. This Butler refused to accept, saying that it would be an injustice to Grant.

As commander of the Army of the James, created for the purpose of co-operating with Grant in the reduction of Richmond, Butler added nothing to his fame. He was hampered and hindered by two unfriendly and disobedient corps commanders, Smith and Gilmore, who thwarted him at every move. He was relieved after the failure before Fort

Fisher and returned to his home at Lowell. A curious instance of how a catch phrase will damn a man was the expression employed by Grant in referring to Butler's movements at Bermuda Hundred, when he said, "His (Butler's) army, though in a position of great security, was as completely shut off from further operations directly against Richmond as if it had been in a bottle strongly corked." When this report was published, "Bottled-Up Butler" was the derisive cry that rang through the land. The illustration about the bottle and the cork had been used by Barnard, Grant's chief of engineers, and Grant adopted it in his report without intending to cast discredit or contempt upon Butler. In his *Memoirs* Grant takes great pains to lift the stigma which he had without intention placed on the name of Butler.

One of the mysteries of the Civil War is the relationship between Grant and Butler. In removing Butler from his command over the Army of the James, Grant claims that when he was absent the command devolved, for the whole army, on Butler, he being the senior major-general. This might have had unfortunate consequences, for the officers had little confidence in him. At Butler's request one of his corps commanders, W. F. Smith, was relieved from his command. A few days afterwards Smith wrote a letter to Senator Foote in which he said that on the first day of July, 1864, Grant said to Butler, "General, that drink of whiskey I took has done me good." He then asked Smith for a drink. Smith produced a bottle and let him have a drink, but did not drink himself nor did he offer one to Butler. After the lapse of an hour, Grant called for the bottle again. When he left, Smith went out "to see him on his horse." When he returned to his tent, an aide said to Smith, "General Grant has gone away drunk; General Butler has seen it, and will never fail to use the weapon which has been put in his hands."

In his *Butler's Book,* Butler denies that any such meeting ever took place. Yet the idea has persisted that in some way Butler had a hold on Grant and prevented him from acting for the best interests of the service. Senator Hoar, in his bitter chapter on Butler, carefully preserves the tradition: "I do not suppose that the secret of the hold which General Butler had upon General Grant will ever be disclosed. Butler boasted in the lobby of the House of Representatives that Grant would not dare to refuse any request of his because he had in his possession affidavits by which he could prove that Grant had been drunk on seven different occasions." When this statement was repeated to Grant by a member of the House, Grant replied quietly, "I have refused his requests several times." Was this an admission or a denial? On his tour around the world Grant said to his companion, John Russell Young, "I liked Butler and always found him, as all the world knows, not only a man of great ability, but a patriotic man, and a man of courage, honor and sincere convictions. Butler is a man it is the fashion to abuse, but he is a man who has done to his country great service and who is worthy of its gratitude."

On November 2, 1864, Butler, in response to a

telegram, appeared at headquarters at the War Department in Washington. Stanton put a bundle of papers in his hands. It was a report of the secret service about an impending outbreak in New York. A prominent army officer was to command the rebellious organization. The Republicans were to be driven from the polls at the election and the whole vote of New York City was to be deposited for McClellan. The report was exaggerated, but the situation was serious. In that crisis the one man of iron nerve and courage to whom the Government turned was Butler. He did his work as well in New York as he had done it in New Orleans. On the day of the election ferryboats lay in the North River and the East River loaded with troops ready to be landed at any point in the city where disorder might break out. The election passed off as quietly as a state fair.

When Butler was in command of the Army of the James he came into collision with the state government of loyal Virginia as exercised by Governor Pierpont, who had moved his capital to Alexandria. In some clash as to the regulations for policing Norfolk, Butler ordered a plebescite, and Pierpont properly protested against this order as usurping the civil rights. In a characteristic arraignment of Pierpont and his state government, Butler described it as a "useless, expensive and inefficient thing, unrecognized by Congress, unknown to the Constitution of the United States, and of such a character that there is no command in the Decalogue against worshiping it, it being in the likeness of nothing in the heavens above or the

earth beneath, or the waters under the earth."
Lincoln wrote him in reply a long and patient letter, in which he cautioned Butler against trespass-
ing on the rights of the civil authorities, and making the very pertinent suggestion that any measure necessary for the health and safety of Norfolk
he should take upon the ground of military necessity, and not submit the matter to a popular vote,
for to do so was to raise the question of its necessity.

One of the last and most interesting meetings
between Lincoln and Butler took place shortly before Lincoln's assassination. During the conversation Lincoln expressed great anxiety about the
negroes when peace should be established. He reverted to his favorite and fantastic idea of transporting the negroes out of the country, saying that
until they were gone, North and South could never
live together in peace. He was especially anxious
about the black soldiers, saying, "If these black
soldiers of ours go back to the South, I am afraid
that they will be but little better off with their
masters than they were before, and yet they will
be free men. I fear a race war, and it will be at
least a guerrilla war because we have taught these
men how to fight. All the arms of the South are
now in the hands of their troops, and when we
capture them of course we take their arms. There
are plenty of men in the North who will furnish
the negroes with arms if there is any oppression
of them by their late masters."

Lincoln then asked Butler to go carefully into
the practicability of transporting the blacks to

some other land, making use of the navy, which at the end of the war would have no employment. The second day thereafter Butler returned with this report: "Mr. President, I have gone carefully over my calculations as to the power of the country to export the negroes of the South, and I assure you that using all your naval vessels and all the merchant marine fit to cross the seas with safety, it will be impossible for you to transport them to the nearest place that can be found fit for them—and that is the Island of San Domingo—half as fast as negro children will be born here." In this Lincoln reluctantly acquiesced. He then asked Butler to suggest some solution of the problem of the negro soldiers. Butler made a very sensible suggestion that they be employed in digging a canal across the Isthmus of Darien between the Atlantic and Pacific and at the same time establish a colony there. Lincoln greeted the idea with his favorite phrase, "There is meat in that," and asked Butler to lay the proposal before Mr. Seward. But before Butler had an opportunity to do this Seward was dangerously injured in a runaway.

Butler would have been President of the United States if Lincoln's first choice of nominee for the Vice-Presidency in the campaign of 1864 had been that of the Convention which met at Baltimore. Hannibal Hamlin had served faithfully and was personally acceptable to Lincoln and the party. But although Hamlin was a Democrat, he was not a "war Democrat," and Lincoln felt that the nomination and election of a strong and aggressive "war Democrat" would greatly strengthen the hands of his administration. He wished, if possible, to de-sectionalize the party and get in its councils some strong and loyal men from a Southern state. With such a man as Vice-President the party would appear more national, and England and France would be less likely to recognize the South. This was why the lot fell on Andrew Johnson, of Tennessee. But Lincoln's first choice was Butler.

In March, 1864, Lincoln dispatched Simon Cameron to visit Butler at Fort Monroe. Cameron said to Butler that Mr. Hamlin would probably not be a candidate for re-election, and that, aside from reasons of personal friendship and esteem, the President would like to have Butler on the ticket with him, for he felt that since Butler was the first prominent Democrat to volunteer for the war, his candidature would greatly strengthen the ticket. To this Butler made one of his characteristic replies: "Please say to Mr. Lincoln that while I appreciate with the fullest sensibility this act of friendship and the compliment he pays me, yet I must decline. Tell him I would not quit the field to be Vice-President, even with himself as President, unless he will give me bond, with sureties, in the full sum of his four years' salary, that he will die or resign within three months after his inauguration." Butler had had intimation that Grant was to give him a high command, the Army of the James, in the operations against Richmond, and thought his chances of service and distinction much greater in the field than in the Vice-President's chair. When Butler facetiously said that he would not take the Vice-Presidency unless Lincoln gave him bond to die or resign within three months after his inauguration, little did he think that he was throwing away his chance to be President of the United States, for just six weeks after Lincoln's inauguration the assassin's bullet vacated the Presidency, and Andrew Johnson became President.*

Butler was born for a riot. Whether handling the election mobs of New York or the secession mobs of New Orleans, he was perfectly at home. He was resourceful, quick, daring, and courageous in the highest degree. I doubt if the conduct of any general in the midst of battle during the war can rank, for sheer courage, moral and physical, with that of Butler on the balcony of the *St. Charles Hotel* before the raging mob that shouted for his blood. He was a real patriot, too. The Government of the United States of America was to him an august reality. A sin against its honor or its flag was to him an unpardonable offense; it called for punishment, and he always sought means to inflict the punishment. Butler was the first to arm the negroes and give them an opportunity to help win their freedom with their own blood.

When you have said these things about Butler you have said the best things. He was arrogant, boastful, bombastic, vindictive, and even vituperative. Probably no serious book ever written by

* In their history of Lincoln, Nicolay and Hay deny that Lincoln expressed any desire in the matter of the Vice-Presidency. But the correspondence published by Col. A. K. McClure in his "Lincoln and Men of War Times" leaves no doubt as to the part played by Lincoln in the shelving of Hannibal Hamlin and the choice of Andrew Johnson.

a person of equal prominence contains so much bitter abuse and unmeasured invective as his autobiography. As a politician it is impossible to locate him or classify him in his frequent changes of front and party. But always he was a fighter. He was the last of the vituperative politicians. There was a strain of coarseness in him. The order against the women of New Orleans was to the point, and immediately effective; but with most of the officers of the Union army it would have been an absolute impossibility. He was of the earth, earthy.

LINCOLN AND McCLELLAN

Speaking one day in the Roman Senate of his great contemporary, Julius Cæsar, Cicero said of him, "Coming generations will dispute over him." Among the leading generals of the Civil War there is none over whom, both during the war and since, there has been so much dispute as over McClellan. The three score years which have elapsed since the beginning of the war have sifted out the merits and character of most of the chief actors on that stage and settled many a controversy. Warren, Buell, Fitz John Porter, have emerged triumphant from the clouds which enveloped their fame, and a satisfactory account can be given of nearly all the chief military and political figures of that troubled day. The one exception is General McClellan. Over him the dispute still rages, and if time has softened the asperities of the debate concerning him, it has not yet shed any clear ray of illumination upon the controversies which gather about his name. To some, McClellan is the prince of egoists, the grand procrastinator, the timid and doubting captain who counted the enemy's numbers and forgot his own. To others, he is a military genius of the first order, the one first-class military mind among all the officers on both sides, but whose power to strike, and in a single campaign end the war, was thwarted by an incapable administration and the intrigue of politicians.

McClellan was the only prominent officer whom

GEORGE BRINTON McCLELLAN

LINCOLN AND McCLELLAN

Lincoln had known well before the war. When McClellan was engineer and vice-president of the Illinois Central Railroad, and Lincoln was one of its counsel, the two men often met in some out-of-the-way county-seat where a case was being tried, and on many a night McClellan sat by the stove in the country tavern and heard Lincoln tell his stories. "He was never at a loss," says McClellan, "and I could never quite make up my mind how many of them he had really heard before, and how many he invented on the spur of the moment. His stories were seldom refined, but were always to the point." Little could these two men have foreseen their future relationship, Lincoln as President, and McClellan as Commander-in-Chief.

George Brinton McClellan, the son of a Philadelphia physician, was born in that city in 1826. After two years in the University of Pennsylvania he was sent to West Point, where he was graduated in 1846. In that same year he went with the army to Mexico and was breveted first lieutenant for gallantry at Churubusco and made a captain after Chapultepec. After the Mexican War he was engaged in army engineering work and exploration. In 1855 he was sent abroad with a military commission to get information on military systems, and while abroad observed the operations of the allied armies in the Crimea. In 1857 McClellan resigned his commission as captain in the army and became the vice-president of the Illinois Central Railroad, and a little later president of the Ohio & Mississippi Railroad, with headquarters at Cincinnati. At the outbreak of the war he was on his way to Harrisburg to receive from Governor Curtin the command of the Pennsylvania troops, but by special request stopped at Columbus to confer with Governor Dennison on Ohio's military situation. Governor Dennison offered him a commission as major-general commanding the three-months Ohio militia. McClellan accepted the offer, and a month afterwards was made a major-general in the United States army and placed in command of the Department of the Ohio, embracing Ohio, Indiana, and Illinois. His brief campaigns in the mountains of western Virginia killed secession in that part of the country and were the first successes which came to the Union arms. After the defeat of Bull Run he was summoned to Washington to take command of the troops in and about the capital.   ·

When he arrived in Washington McClellan found everything in confusion. The loud cry of "On to Richmond" had been silenced. Streets, hotels and bar-rooms were filled with drunken officers and men absent without leave from their regiments. No proper steps had been taken to secure the safety of the city and no strong mind was guiding or controlling. Into this scene of chaos and pandemonium came the young commander from the mountains of Virginia, quietly giving his orders, riding day and night through his far flung camps, organizing his staff, drilling the regiments which, at the rate of one a day, came pouring in from the loyal states, laying out a system of impregnable defenses for the city, and wherever he went, inspiring confidence and winning the hearts of men.

LINCOLN AND McCLELLAN

Had McClellan never done anything else but organize the Army of the Potomac and bring order out of chaos after the battle of Bull Run, his service to the nation would have been not far behind that of any of the Union generals. The weapon which Grant finally used to strike down the Confederacy was the finely tempered sword of McClellan, the Army of the Potomac. The finest tribute that can be paid to the creative and organizing ability of McClellan is the history of the Army of the Potomac; how it survived disaster after disaster in the field, unbroken in spirit and undiminished in power to strike. Many waters of adversity and floods of defeat could not quench its magnificent spirit.

McClellan was only thirty-five when he was called to his high post in Washington, and it was not strange that his sudden rise to fame, with the devotion of a great army, the deference of statesmen and the plaudits of the press, had a deleterious effect upon his mind. Of such effect there can be no doubt. The unwise publication of his private correspondence as a part of his *McClellan's Own Story* shows plainly the unfortunate effect that his great popularity and pre-eminent position were having upon him. Such sentiments as these we find appearing in his letters: "I find myself in a new and strange position here; President, Cabinet and General Scott, and all deferring to me. By some strange operation of magic I seem to have become the power of the land; ... All tell me that I am responsible for the fate of the nation; ... I am weary of all this; I have .no ambition in the present affairs; only wish to serve my country, and find the incapables around me will not permit it. They sit on the verge of the precipice, and cannot realize what they see." McClellan truly thought that the government was made up of "incapables" and that only a military mind and administrator could save the situation. The fatal mistake he made was in holding himself aloof from those in authority and antagonizing them.

His first quarrel was with the aged and infirm Scott. In this McClellan was not wholly to blame, and no one today will deny that Lincoln ought to have made him commander-in-chief at once, for the incapacity of Scott was apparent to all. On the day that McClellan first arrived at Washington, at his first meeting with Scott he excused himself after a brief interview, saying that the President had asked him to meet the Cabinet at one o'clock. To this Scott took indignant exception, saying that the President had no right to give McClellan such an invitation to his exclusion. This was a sample of what was to follow. McClellan took what was probably the only practical course and completely ignored the Commander-in-Chief, until the old veteran accepted the inevitable and resigned his post. This was in October, and during the three months he had been in Washington McClellan had shown such a grasp of the situation and such a genius for command and organization that Lincoln and the whole nation hailed his elevation to the chief command with delight.

This new honor did not do anything to lessen McClellan's extravagant estimate of the part he must play in saving the Union. So exalted was he that he committed almost unbelievable acts of arrogance and disrespect towards those in high office, and even towards the President of the United States. Lincoln, in his friendly way, came often to McClellan's house. On one occasion when he called he found the General absent at the wedding of an officer. The President sat down in the reception room to wait for his return. After an hour had passed McClellan returned and, disregarding what the orderly said to him about the presence of Lincoln, passed upstairs to his rooms. After a time the President sent a servant to his rooms to announce him again. The servant returned with the words that the General had gone to bed. Mr. Lincoln never asked for an explanation and seemed not to resent this extraordinary conduct. On another occasion when an important conference had been kept waiting through the absence of McClellan, some of those present showed impatience and displeasure at the delay, whereupon Lincoln remarked, "Never mind; I will hold McClellan's horse if he will only bring us success." Undoubtedly many of Lincoln's future troubles with McClellan were due to the fact that he had been too lenient and indulgent towards him in the beginning, and had not sufficiently impressed upon his mind that in a republic the civil authority is supreme.

As the summer faded into autumn, and the autumn into winter, and still nothing was done by the Army of the Potomac, the nation became restive and apprehensive. This dissatisfaction was reflected in the act of Congress appointing a Committee on the Conduct of the War, one of the most important bodies of the whole conflict. This committee began to press Lincoln with complaints against McClellan, insistent that the army do something. None was more anxious for this than Lincoln, but for a period he loyally backed up McClellan and shielded him from the rising storm of protest and unrest, telling members of Congress that McClellan was making sure that all was ready before he moved the army, lest the mistake of Bull Run should be repeated. But the President himself was beginning to have his doubts. He was one day at the telegraph office in the War Department when a despatch came in saying that there had been no firing on McClellan's front since sunset. Lincoln inquired in his whimsical way if there had been any firing *before* sunset, and then related one of his characteristic anecdotes about a man who went around telling of a natural prodigy, a child who was black from his hips down. Asked what color the child was from his hips up, he responded, "Why, black, of course."

In December McClellan fell ill with typhoid fever and was incapacitated for a number of weeks. It was at this time that Lincoln began his serious study of the military situation, reading works on war and studying the maps and fields of operation. His inquiries of Halleck and Buell, the two commanders in the West, revealed to him the startling fact that both of these men were depending upon McClellan for orders and that neither of them contemplated co-operative action; therefore the whole military machine, east and west, was at a standstill. As McClellan's illness showed no signs of abatement, Lincoln summoned to the White House General McDowell and General Franklin and sought their advice about a campaign, saying that if McClellan did not want to use the Army of the Potomac, he would like to borrow it. McDowell advocated a forward move against Johnston's army at Manassas, Franklin an attack upon Richmond by the peninsula between the York and James Rivers, the plan finally adopted by McClellan. A second meeting was held, and a third was arranged for on Sunday, January 13th. At this meeting there were present also three members of the Cabinet, Blair, Chase, and Seward. Meanwhile McClellan had got word of these conferences and made a dramatic appearance at the one held on the 13th at the White House. There was a good deal of embarrassment and awkward whisperings among those present until Lincoln asked McDowell to state what they had been doing, and what had been proposed. McDowell did so, at the same time in a courteous way disclaiming any hostility towards McClellan, and saying that what had been done was in view of the supposed critical illness of the Commander-in-Chief. In a cold and curt manner McClellan interrupted him, saying that as he had again been restored to health there was no further need of examination into the proposed movements of the army. Then Franklin made a disclaimer of any disloyalty to McClellan, and the whispering recommenced, especially between the President and Secretary Chase. At length, manifesting great excitement and irritation, Chase asked McClellan to state what he intended to do with the Army of the Potomac. McClellan answered that he did not recognize the Secretary of the Treasury as his official superior and denied his right to question him upon military affairs, and that to the President and the Secretary of War alone would he confide his plans. McClellan then resumed his conversation with Blair, paying no further attention to the angry Chase. The latter whispered for a few minutes with the President, and then Lincoln said, in a conciliatory tone, "Well, General McClellan, I think you had better tell us what your plans are." To this McClellan responded that if the President had confidence in him it was not necessary that he should entrust his designs to the judgment of others, and that he would give out no further information at the meeting unless ordered to do so by the President in writing. Lincoln then asked him if in his own mind he had any particular time set for a movement of the army. Upon McClellan answering in the affirmative, Lincoln said, "Then I will adjourn this meeting." But according to McClellan's version of this memorable day, the meeting was adjourned by Seward getting up and, as he buttoned his coat, saying, "Well, Mr. President, I think the meeting had better break up. I don't see that we are likely to make much out of General McClellan."

McClellan had gained knowledge of these conferences during his illness through Stanton, not yet Secretary of War, who said to him, "They are counting on your death, and are already dividing among themselves your military goods and chattels." McClellan was altogether within his rights in refusing to divulge his plans except to the President and Secretary of War, but he seems to have forgotten that he was in conference with able and patriotic men occupying high positions of responsibility, all earnest in their efforts to preserve the Union. His attitude towards them was certainly anything but conciliatory, and from that day one powerful member of the Cabinet, Chase, was his relentless foe. From the evidence at hand McClellan was unjust in his suspicions that McDowell had been zealous in these private conferences with the President with the hope that he would succeed him in command.

From this time on there was a more or less organized warfare on McClellan from the rear. Stanton, who had entered the Cabinet as the friend of McClellan, became his most determined enemy. Worst of all, McClellan, about to embark upon the great movement against the enemy, was convinced in his mind that the radical element in the administration was determined to undo him and keep him from being successful in his campaign. "Had I been successful," writes McClellan, "in my first campaign, the rebellion would perhaps have been terminated without the immediate abolition of slavery. I believe that the leaders of the radical branch of the Republican party preferred political control in one section of a divided country to being in the minority in a restored Union. Not only did these people desire the abolition of slavery, but its abolition in such a manner and under such circumstances that the slaves would be at once endowed with the electoral franchise, and permanent control thus be secured through the votes of the ignorant slaves, composing so large a portion of the population of the seceded states. Influenced by these motives they succeeded but too well in sowing the seeds of distrust in Mr. Lincoln's mind, so that, even before I actually commenced the Peninsular campaign, I had lost the cordial support of the executive which was necessary to certain success." If he felt that way when he was about to commence his campaign, was it not McClellan's duty, it will be asked, to resign the command? McClellan's answer to this is the following: "It may be said that under these circumstances it was my duty to resign my command. But I had become warmly attached to the soldiers, who already had learned to love me well; all my pride was wrapped up in the army that I had created, and I knew no commander at all likely to be assigned to it in my place who could be competent to conduct its operations. Nor did I at that time fully realize the length to which these men were prepared to go in carrying out their schemes. For instance, I did not suspect, until the orders reached me, that Fort Monroe and the 1st Corps would be withdrawn from my control; and when those orders arrived they found me too far committed to permit me to withdraw with honor. With the troops under fire it did not become me to offer my resignation."

After the meeting at the White House, on January 13, 1862, Lincoln waited patiently for a number of weeks, and as there was still no sign of

activity on the part of McClellan's army he issued
his General Order No. 1, directing a forward movement by land and sea of all the forces of the army
and the navy on February 22d. McClellan con-
trived to disobey this order, but did put into execution an abortive movement towards Winchester by
way of Harper's Ferry. The movement failed because at the last moment it was discovered that the
canal boats which had been collected, and with
which a permanent bridge was to have been constructed at Harper's Ferry, were too large to pass
through the lift-lock into the river. It was when
an officer reported to him this fiasco and told him
that the movement had been arrested because the
pontoons were not ready, that the sorely tried
Lincoln for once lost his patience and, relapsing
into the provincialism of the frontier, said in a
voice of thunder to the astonished officer, "Why
in h—l ain't they ready?"

This was in substance the question which was
everywhere being asked in the North. At the early
hour of seven o'clock on the 8th of March, Lincoln
summoned McClellan to his office and said that
he wished to speak to him about a "very ugly
matter." Then followed one of the most dramatic
scenes of the war. The "ugly matter" was the
rumor that McClellan's plan of campaign for attacking Richmond by way of the Peninsula was
conceived with the traitorous intent of removing
its defenders from Washington and thus giving
over to the enemy the capital and the government.
Lincoln concluded by saying that it looked to him
very much like treason. With that McClellan

sprang to his feet and demanded that Lincoln with-draw the expression, that he could not permit any one to couple the word treason with his name. Lincoln, in great agitation, assured McClellan that he was only repeating what he had heard and what he himself did not believe. He finally succeeded in pacifying the outraged McClellan and they parted with mutual good understanding. It is painful to recall this interview between Lincoln and McClellan. The President virtually charges the Commander-in-Chief with treasonable designs on the eve of his campaign. There is no question that McClellan's now numerous enemies were saying that he was not loyal to the Government, but that Lincoln, convinced or unconvinced in his own mind, should have thus brought the matter to McClellan's attention is well-nigh inconceivable. In extenuation of the President's action it may be said that his heart was eaten with anxiety for the safety of the nation, and men high in the Government were hinting at the disloyalty of the Commander-in-Chief of the armies.

When McClellan finally got under way for the Peninsula, it was reported to Lincoln that he had left only nineteen thousand troops for the defense of the capital. One of the conditions upon which Lincoln consented to the Peninsular plan of campaign was that McClellan should leave behind sufficient troops to defend Washington. Lincoln therefore held back from McClellan the first corps of his army, McDowell's. In this Lincoln acted with sincere, though unwarranted, anxiety for the safety of Washington. But McClellan took it as another evidence of the plot of his enemies to ruin him. From the time that he landed on the Peninsula until he was driven back to Harrison's Landing, after the Seven Days' Battle, McClellan sent to Washington unceasing demands for more men and unceasing complaints that the Government was not supporting him. These demands induced the irritable Stanton to exclaim one day, "If he had a million men he would swear the enemy had two million men, and then would sit down in the mud and yell for another million." This hyperbole of Stanton's reveals McClellan's weakness of always overrating the forces opposed to him, and shows the contempt in which Stanton now held him.

To McClellan's complaining dispatches Lincoln answered with kind and patient words, saying, "Your dispatches complaining that you are not properly sustained, while they do not offend me, do pain me very much. I beg to assure you that I have never written you or spoken to you in greater kindness of feeling than now, nor with a fuller purpose to sustain you, so far as in my anxious judgment, I consistently can. But you must act." Yet partly through the fears of the Government, and partly through Lincoln's effort to capture "Stonewall" Jackson through a strategic movement of his own, the much disputed-over 1st Corps was held back from McClellan's army. When it was too late for it to come to the rescue, Lee and Jackson had attacked McClellan's right flank and the desperate Seven Days' Battle was on.

A bolder general than McClellan might have elected to advance towards Richmond after the first repulse of the Confederate attack. Instead of this McClellan chose to change his base from the York River to the James. This retrograde movement was a masterpiece of military strategy and the behavior of the army was magnificent. As he fought his way by day and by night through the swamps and jungles of the Peninsula, McClellan's dispatches indicated that he felt more bitterly towards his own Government than he did toward the foe hanging on his rear. This bitterness and disappointment reached its climax of expression in the amazing dispatch which McClellan sent to Stanton from Savage Station on the 28th of June, after the battle of Gaines' Mill. In this dispatch McClellan said, "I have lost this battle because my force was too small. If at this instant I could dispose of ten thousand fresh men, I could gain a victory tomorrow. I know that a few thousand more men would have changed this battle from a defeat to a victory. I feel too earnestly tonight; I have seen too many dead and wounded comrades to feel otherwise than that the Government has not sustained this army. If you do not do so now, the game is lost. If I save this army now, I tell you plainly that I owe no thanks to you or to any other persons in Washington. You have done your best to sacrifice this army."

The thrust of this message was meant for Stanton, but it included the President also. Lincoln's distress during the time of McClellan's retreat down the Peninsula was very great, for the dispatches of McClellan indicated that the destruction or the capitulation of the army was not an improbability. He sent encouraging messages to McClellan exhorting him to "save the army." This McClellan did in masterly fashion and the retreat across the Peninsula to Harrison's Landing was, as he himself termed it, a "magnificent episode," though not the kind of episode which puts down a rebellion and wins peace.

When the army was at length safe under the protection of the gunboats at Harrison's Landing, Lincoln went down to visit the troops and encourage his general. While he was there McClellan delivered to him a long letter which he had addressed to him on the conduct of civil and military matters. In this impudent and presumptuous document McClellan undertook to explain to the President his duties, how private property and unarmed persons are to be protected, how slavery must not be forcibly interferred with, and how the army needed a commander-in-chief who should enjoy the confidence of the President. Lincoln read the letter, put it in his pocket, and never referred to it again. It was a letter well worthy of being placed side by side with that which Seward wrote Lincoln at the beginning of the war. McClellan still assured Lincoln that he could take Richmond if given more men. His army had already swallowed up so many reinforcements that Lincoln remarked that sending reinforcements to McClellan was like "shoveling fleas across a barnyard—not half of them got there."

McClellan's hint about the necessity of a commander-in-chief was soon to be acted upon by the President, but not in the way McClellan had supposed. When McClellan was about to take the field against Richmond, Lincoln, without warning, removed him from the chief command, leaving him commander of the Army of the Potomac. This was a military blunder of the first order and had an unhappy effect upon the campaign which followed. Instead of one army operating against the enemy in Virginia, and under one supreme command, there were several armies acting independently. A letter of General Keyes, commander of the 4th Army Corps, to Senator Ira Harris, and given to the President, sums up the weakness of the military situation. In this letter, written at Warwick Courthouse, on April 7, 1862, General Keyes says, "The plan of campaign on this line was made with the distinct understanding that *four* army corps should be employed. Today I have learned that the 1st Army Corps and one division of the 2nd Army Corps have been withdrawn altogether from this line of operations. The greatest master of the art of war said that 'If you would invade a country successfully, you must have one line of operations and one army under one general.' But what is our condition? The State of Virginia is made to constitute the command, in part or wholly, of some six generals, viz.: Fremont, Banks, McDowell, Wool, Burnside, and McClellan."

This was indeed the fatal weakness of the campaign. Even before the reverse on the Peninsula, Lincoln must have realized that something was wrong, for in the latter part of June he made his secret visit to General Scott at West Point and sought his advice on the management of the armies. Scott advised him to return McDowell's corps to McClellan, and it is supposed that it was he who suggested Halleck as commander-in-chief. On July 11th Halleck was made commander-in-chief and reported at Washington. After a visit to McClellan's army at Harrison's Landing he advocated its withdrawal and its union with the Army of Virginia, now under Pope. In this the Government acquiesced and, against McClellan's earnest protest, withdrew his army from the Peninsula. Few students of the war will deny that this was a great blunder. Properly backed up, McClellan could have taken Richmond and ended the war. His protest against the withdrawal of his army was prophetic, for he said, "Here is the true defense of Washington. It is here on the banks of the James that the fate of the Union should be decided." And so it proved to be, for Grant, after his fruitless struggles through the wilderness towards Richmond and the bloody repulse at Cold Harbor, abandoned the plan along which he said he would fight it out if it took all summer—that of throwing his army against the right flank of Lee and trying to get between him and Richmond —and taking his army to the James River, commenced where McClellan had left off two years before.

During the battle of Second Bull Run McClellan, not removed from his command, but with his army taken away from him and given to Pope, sat in his tent at Alexandria and heard the thunder of the guns, in vain beseeching his Government to let him share in the fight, finally saying, "I cannot express to you the pain and mortification I have experienced today in listening to the distant sound of the firing of my men. As I can be of no further use here I respectfully ask that, if there is a probability of the conflict being renewed tomorrow, I may be permitted to go to the scene of the battle with my staff, merely to be with my own men, if nothing more; they will fight none the worse for my being with them. If it is not deemed best to entrust me with the command even of my own army, I simply ask to be permitted to share their fate on the field of battle." The next day the battle was renewed but without the help or presence of McClellan, and the Union army by nightfall was in full retreat upon Washington.

The next chapter in McClellan's history reads like a romance. As the disastrous battle goes against the Union army, he sits impatient and disconsolate in his tent at Alexandria, a discredited and apparently forgotten general, of whose services the army and the Government have no need. Within two days after we see him called by his Government into the field again to save the capital and turn defeat into victory. Late at night, on the 31st of August, the mentally paralyzed Halleck telegraphed McClellan for his aid in the crisis, adding that he was "utterly played out." McClellan went the next day to Washington and advised the immediate withdrawal of Pope's beaten army to the fortifications. Halleck issued these orders and gave McClellan verbal command over the troops for the defense of Washington. At seven o'clock the next morning Halleck and Lincoln called at McClellan's home. Lincoln, betraying great emotion, said he regarded Washington as lost and asked McClellan if he would "under the circumstances, as a favor to him, resume command and do the best that could be done." McClellan accepted the grave responsibility and immediately set about the disposition of the troops for the defense of the capital. In a few days he had accomplished the miracle of reorganization, and the army was in pursuit of Lee, who had crossed the Potomac in his invasion of Maryland.

Lincoln never fronted such a storm of criticism and opposition as when he restored McClellan to the command of the army. In Congress and in the Cabinet the feeling against McClellan was most intense. General Pope attributed his ill success to the non-support of McClellan and his generals, and this impression prevailed throughout the country. On August 29th, Chase, the Secretary of the Treasury, presented to Gideon Welles, the Secretary of the Navy, a petition to the President asking for the removal of McClellan and citing grave charges against him. Welles himself was unfavorable to McClellan, but declined to sign the paper. Three days later Chase presented to him a second paper, but more moderate than the former, stating that the Cabinet did not believe McClellan should be intrusted with the command of the army. Since the former paper had been presented the Union army had been worsted at Second Bull Run, and the enemies of McClellan, knowing that the army must have a new commander, were apprehensive lest McClellan should be recalled. Welles too hoped that McClellan would not be put in command, but refused to sign the paper, saying that it was a wrong way of seeking to influence the choice of the President. "It was evident," writes Welles, "there was a fixed determination to remove, and if possible, to disgrace McClellan. Chase frankly stated he deserved it, that he deliberately believed McClellan ought to be shot, and should, were he President, be brought to summary punishment."

Postmaster-General Blair, writing in 1879 of the intrigue against McClellan, says, "The folly and disregard of public interests thus exhibited would be incredible, but that the authors of this intrigue, Messrs. Stanton and Chase, when the result of it came, and I proposed the restoration of McClellan to command, to prevent the completion of ruin by the fall of this capital, actually declared that they would prefer the loss of the capital to the restoration of McClellan to command."

There was a stormy scene at the meeting of the Cabinet on September 2nd, when Lincoln announced that McClellan had been restored to command. In answer to the reproaches of Stanton and Chase and the protests of most of the other members of the Cabinet, Lincoln declared that he had acted for the best interests of the country, that while McClellan had the "slows," and was good for nothing for a forward movement, none could surpass him in the defensive and as an organizer, and that he was thoroughly familiar with the whole ground to be occupied by the army. When Chase declared that giving McClellan command was equivalent to giving Washington to the rebels, Lincoln answered that he was distressed to find himself in disagreement with the Secretary of War and the Secretary of the Treasury, and that he would gladly resign his place. So ended what Welles describes as the most agitated and despondent meeting the Cabinet ever held.

Why was it that Lincoln, who above all others had reason to be displeased with McClellan, restored him to the command in face of the opposition of the Cabinet and Congress and the hostile sentiment of the country? The first reason was the military ability of McClellan to cope with the critical situation which had arisen in the fortunes of the army and the nation. Whatever the Cabinet and Congress thought of McClellan, there could be no doubt as to what the army thought of him. Lincoln knew that the officers and the men loved him and would follow him. He knew, too, of McClellan's great gift for organizing an army and putting a fighting spirit into it, and the retreat through the Peninsula had established the fame of McClellan as a great defensive general. Lincoln counted over his generals and asked himself which one of them could meet the emergency—Halleck, rubbing his elbows and smoking his cigar, and calling for McClellan to aid him? Pope, beaten and discredited? McDowell, twice beaten at Bull Run, and so disliked by the troops that after Second Bull Run it was not safe for him to visit the camps of his men, who declared that they would kill him? There were indeed officers like Meade, who had the engineering ability to defend the capital, but none of them had the personal magnetism which was now required for bringing together the defeated and dispirited army. The finger of destiny pointed to McClellan. Lincoln swallowed his own pride and mortification, and for the sake of the cause, which was ever uppermost in his mind, asked the man whom but a few days before he had permitted to be stripped of his army, to resume the command. It was one of the most important and patriotic acts of Lincoln's administration of the war. To Gideon Welles, the Secretary of the Navy, Lincoln said, "I must have McClellan to reorganize the army and bring it out of chaos. But there has been a design, a purpose in breaking down Pope, without regard of consequences to the country. It is shocking to see and know this; but there is no remedy at present, McClellan has the army with him." To another Lincoln said, "There is no one in the army who can man these fortifications and lick these troops of ours into shape half as well as he can. We must use the tools we have; if he cannot fight himself, he excels in making others ready to fight."

The second reason for the restoration of McClellan was political; that is, it was done with regard to the feeling of the people of the North. The progress of the war was bringing McClellan out as the foremost figure in the Democratic party. Lincoln felt the necessity of having the support of all elements of the people in the crisis confronting him, and knew that while the restoration of McClellan would offend radical Republicans it would please all the Democrats.

The splendid reception which the army gave

LINCOLN AND McCLELLAN

McClellan when he returned to take command proved that Lincoln was right and his Cabinet wrong. An officer of the Union army, Captain John D. Wilkins, tells how, on the evening of September 2, 1862, he was marching along with the dispirited host which was streaming towards Washington. The troops had halted and were lying on the ground resting, when, in the gathering gloom, Wilkins saw two horsemen approaching from the opposite direction. A second glance at the trim military figure on one of the horses told him who it was and he shouted to his colonel, "McClellan is here!" At the sound of that name the weary soldiers leaped to their feet and a roar of cheering passed like a wave over companies, regiments, brigades, divisions, corps, until the remotest units of this great host caught up the tumultuous refrain. Unstrung by the terrible experiences of the past two days, many of the soldiers broke from the ranks and crowded about McClellan's horse, crying like children, praising God for his return, and calling upon him to lead them once more against the foe.

In the short and brilliant campaign which ended in the battle of Antietam, McClellan more than fulfilled the hopes which were reposed in him. The capital was saved, and Lee, with a beaten and sadly depleted army, had retreated into Virginia. Lincoln celebrated the victory by the first proclamation of emancipation. In the presumptuous letter which he had addressed to Lincoln earlier in the summer McClellan had expressed his opposition to the measure and his dread of its results.

When he heard of the proclamation McClellan wrote to his wife, "The President's late proclamation, and the continuance in office of Stanton and Halleck, render it almost impossible for me to retain my commission and self-respect at the same time." General W. F. Smith is authority for the statement that McClellan prepared a protest against the proclamation and read it to some of his friends in the army, who dissuaded him from publishing it. Instead, with due respect to the President and the civil authorities, McClellan issued an address to the army in which he asked their support of the Government and advised them to restrain from intemperate discussion of public measures determined upon by those in authority.

On the first of October Lincoln paid a visit to the army at Antietam and remained with McClellan for seven days. During this visit McClellan received the impression that Lincoln was quite satisfied with his conduct of the campaign, and would stand by him to the last. He said to McClellan that the only fault he had to find with him was that he was "too prone to be sure that everything was ready before starting." To this McClellan rejoined that the experiments Lincoln had had with those who acted before they were ready ought to convince him that he consumed less time than they did. "He repeated that he was entirely satisfied with me," wrote McClellan, "that I should be let alone; that he would stand by me. I have no doubt that he meant exactly what he said. He parted from me with the utmost cordiality. We never met again on this earth." But as soon as

LINCOLN AND McCLELLAN

Lincoln reached Washington McClellan began to be pressed with orders for an immediate advance into Virginia. It was after this visit to McClellan's headquarters at Antietam that some one spoke to Lincoln about McClellan's great capacity as a military engineer. "Yes," answered Lincoln, "McClellan is a great engineer, but his specialty seems to be a stationary engine." Now that the crisis was safely over, Chase and Stanton and the other enemies of McClellan resumed their warfare in his rear. On September 22nd McClellan wrote in prophetic words to his wife, "It may be, now that the Government is pretty well over their scare, they will begin again with their persecutions and throw me overboard again." So it proved to be.

If the restoration of McClellan to the command of the army was one of the most fearless and patriotic acts of Abraham Lincoln, his removal of McClellan from that post after the victorious campaign of Antietam was one of the most unfortunate acts of his administration and one for which there was the least excuse. McClellan attributed his removal to the cabal against him on the part of Chase and Stanton; but in the end Lincoln must be held responsible, for he had once before defied the wishes of these enemies of McClellan and could have done so again. When he restored McClellan to the command of the army Lincoln had made reference to the employment of McClellan's abilities in the crisis at that time facing the Government. In view of what followed, it is probable that Lincoln did not propose that McClellan should be the leader of the next great offensive of the army. Antietam changed the national situation; the administration saw itself strong and secure, and the Proclamation of Emancipation had added immensely to the prestige and power of Lincoln. At all events, Lincoln felt that he was strong enough to dispense with the services of McClellan, if he thought it wise to do so. This he did on November 7, 1862, just after McClellan had crossed the Potomac and was advancing against Lee's army. General Burnside was placed in command of the army and McClellan ordered to repair to Trenton, N. J., to "await further orders" which never came. The removal was a hard blow to McClellan and created intense resentment in the army, so that not a few advised McClellan to ignore the order, march upon Washington, and take possession of the Government. There is no doubt that he could have done so, so deep was the attachment of the army to him. But like a true patriot McClellan turned over the command to Burnside and assisted him in every way possible to get the situation in hand.

McClellan was as happy in his dispatches and orders as he was in personal contact. His farewell message to the army shows him at his best in this respect: "In parting from you I cannot express the love and gratitude I bear to you. As an army you have grown up under my care. In you I have never found doubt or coldness. The battles you have fought under my command will proudly live in our nation's history. The glory you have achieved, our mutual perils and fatigues, the graves of our comrades fallen in battle and by disease, the broken forms of those whom wounds and sickness have disabled—the strongest associations which can exist among men—unite us still by an indissoluble tie."

During the remaining years of the war McClellan occupied the place of prominence and influence to which his great services entitled him, although never again having any part in the military operations. The summer of 1863 was a very anxious one for the administration of Lincoln, and in June of that year Thurlow Weed planned a great meeting in New York in support of the war and the Union. He knew that it would add immensely to the meeting if McClellan were present, and he went to the General and invited him to preside. McClellan at first consented, but at the last moment declined. In the summer of 1864 he was nominated for the Presidency by the Democratic convention at Chicago with its infamous platform which declared the war to be a failure and hinted at compromise with the South. McClellan's speech of acceptance repudiated the shameful platform, and he came out strongly for the Union, but this could not save him from overwhelming defeat at the polls in November. Atlanta, Mobile Bay, and Winchester were victories which knocked the props from under the Democratic platform and its celebrated candidate. Before the nomination of McClellan by the Democrats, his old and firm friend, Postmaster-General Blair, went to McClellan and sought to secure his support of the administration. He urged him to have nothing to do with the Chicago convention, telling him that defeat was certain. Instead of the miserable portion of a defeated candidate for the Presidency, Blair held out before McClellan the nobler lot of rallying to the support of the Union party the loyal Democrats of the North. His suggestion was that McClellan write a letter to Lincoln asking to be restored to a command in the army. One could wish that McClellan had accepted Blair's advice. But McClellan knew that his military fame was secure, he had had experience with the opposition of the Government to him as a commander, and, no doubt, had hopes of success as the Democratic candidate in the forthcoming election.

Before the victories of Atlanta, Mobile Bay, and Winchester, Lincoln expected defeat. On the 23rd of August, several days before the meeting of the convention which nominated McClellan, Lincoln wrote the following vow: "This morning, as for some days past, it seems exceedingly probable that this administration will not be re-elected. Then it will be my duty to so co-operate with the President-elect as to save the Union between the election and the inauguration; as he will have secured his election on such ground that he cannot possibly save it afterwards." He had the members of the Cabinet endorse this statement by writing their names across the back of the paper, though they knew not what it contained. His purpose was to pledge the administration to accept the verdict of the people at the polls and do all they could to save the Union before they went out of office. After his victory at the polls Lincoln read the contents of the paper to the Cabinet and said that if McClellan had been elected he would have sent for him and said to him, "General, the election has demonstrated that you are stronger, have more influence with the American people than I. Now let us together, you with your influence, and I with all the executive power of the Government, try to save the country. You raise as many troops as you possibly can for this final trial, and I will devote all energies to assist and finish the war." When he was through, Seward said to him, "And the General would have answered you, 'Yes, yes,' and the next day when you saw him again and pressed these views upon him he would have said, 'Yes, yes,' and so on forever and would have done nothing at all."

So, with this final fling against him for his habit of procrastination and delay, the great soldier passed forever out of the counsels of Lincoln and his Cabinet.

LINCOLN AND SHERMAN

Like most of the officers who rose to prominence during the war, Sherman had resigned his commission in the regular army and had been in civil life for a number of years when hostilities broke out. After leaving the army in 1853 he engaged for a time in banking in San Francisco, conducted a business in New York, tried his hand at law in Kansas, and in 1860 became the head of the State Military College of Louisiana. When it became evident that Louisiana would secede from the Union, Sherman resigned his post and went north. Early in March, 1861, he went to Washington to visit his brother John, the Senator from Ohio. He accompanied his brother to the White House and met Lincoln for the first time. When Senator Sherman had finished his business with the President he said to him, "Mr. President, this is my brother, Colonel Sherman, who is just up from Louisiana; he may give you some information you want." To this Lincoln responded, "Ah! how are they getting along down there?" Sherman answered, "They think they are getting along swimmingly—they are preparing for war." "Oh, well!" said Lincoln, "I guess we'll manage to keep house." Sherman felt that he had been snubbed, and was sadly disappointed in the attitude of Lincoln and others in authority at Washington. What particularly displeased Sherman was Lincoln's adding, "I guess we'll get along without you fellows," mean-

WILLIAM TECUMSEH SHERMAN

ing that he thought there would be no war. As
they went out from the interview Sherman said
to his brother, "You (meaning the politicians)
have got things in a hell of a fix, and you may
get them out as best you can."

From Washington Sherman went to St. Louis to
take the presidency of a street railway and watch
the drift of events. Although he was disgusted
with the administration, and had told his brother
he would have nothing to do with the Government's efforts to save the country, he thought better of it and wrote to the Secretary of War offer-
ing his services, not as a three-months man but as
a three-years man. To this somewhat haughty
letter he received no reply, but on the 14th of
May, 1861, was appointed Colonel of the Thirteenth Regular Infantry. He was put in command
of a brigade in McDowell's army and shared in the
debacle of Bull Run. His next meeting with Lincoln was shortly after that battle. He saw the
President and Secretary Seward riding in a carriage and asked them if they were going to his
camps. To this Lincoln responded, "Yes; we
heard that you had got over the big scare, and we
thought we would come over and see the 'boys'."
Sherman asked if he might give the coachman
directions as to the best road to the camps and was
invited by the President to get in and ride with
them. As they drew near the camp, Sherman saw
that the President was full of feeling and wanted
to encourage the men. He asked him if he intended
to make a speech, and upon being told that he
would like to do so, Sherman requested him to

discourage all cheering, noise or any sort of confusion; the army had had enough of it before Bull Run to ruin any set of men, and what the army needed was cool, thoughtful and fighting soldiers —"no more hurrahing, no more humbug." Lincoln took this somewhat presumptuous advice of Sherman's in good part, and when some of the men began to cheer, he checked them, saying as he did so, "Don't cheer, boys. I confess I rather like it myself, but Colonel Sherman here says it is not military, and I guess we had better defer to his opinion."

On the morning of the day of this visit of Lincoln, an officer of one of the three-months regiments whose time was up had said to Sherman, "Colonel, I am going to New York today. What can I do for you?" Sherman asked him how he could go, for he did not remember having signed a leave for him. The officer answered that he did not require a leave; he had enlisted for three months and his time was up, and he could no longer neglect his business. Leave or no leave, he was going that day to New York. A large group of soldiers stood about listening to this conversation, and realizing that it was a critical situation, Sherman turned on the man and said with great severity, at the same time feeling in the breast of his overcoat, "Captain, this question of your term of service has been submitted to the rightful authority and the decision has been published in orders. You are a soldier and must submit to orders till you are properly discharged. If you attempt to leave without orders, it will be mutiny, and I will shoot you like a dog! Go back into the fort *now,* instantly, and don't dare to leave it without my consent." The officer promptly obeyed and the men dispersed.

After the President had concluded his speech to the men at Fort Corcoran, Sherman observed this same officer approaching the carriage where he sat with Lincoln and Seward. When he was at the side of the carriage the officer said to Lincoln, "Mr. President, I have a cause of grievance (the President had ended his speech by inviting them to appeal to him in person if they had any cause of complaint). This morning I went to speak to Colonel Sherman, and he threatened to shoot me." Mr. Lincoln, who was still standing in the carriage from which he had been speaking to the men, said, "Threatened to shoot you?" "Yes, sir," replied the officer, "he threatened to shoot me." Looking from the officer to Sherman, and from Sherman back to the officer, Lincoln stooped down towards the man and said to him in a whisper loud enough to be heard for some distance around the carriage, "Well, if I were you, and he threatened to shoot, I would not trust him, for I believe he would do it." Amid the laughter of the men the officer turned and walked away. When the carriage had gone some distance Lincoln said to Sherman, "Of course, I didn't know anything about it, but I thought you knew your business best." Sherman thanked him for his confidence and told him what he had done would be a great help in maintaining discipline in the somewhat unruly army.

With General McClellan commanding in the East

and Fremont in the Mississippi Valley, no adequate provision had been made for the middle territory and the safety of Kentucky and Tennessee. The Kentucky legislature was in session and ready to act for the Union if backed up by the Government with troops. To meet this situation the Department of the Cumberland was created with Brigadier-General Robert Anderson in command. He chose Sherman as one of his assistants, Sherman having served under him at Fort Moultrie from 1843 to 1846. Lincoln himself came to the *Willard Hotel* and had a conference with Sherman and Anderson, for this territory of Kentucky and Tennessee was always close to the heart of the President.

It was at this conference that Sherman persuaded Lincoln to appoint George H. Thomas a brigadier general. Sherman and Thomas had been classmates at West Point. When General Anderson made a request for Thomas to serve with him as a brigadier-general, Lincoln, cautious by reason of his experience with other Southern-born officers who had gone over to the Confederacy, raised the question as to the loyalty of Thomas to the Union cause, he being a Virginian. Sherman, however, was most emphatic in his endorsement of Thomas, saying to the President, "Old Tom is as loyal as I am!" Largely upon this assurance from Sherman, Lincoln sent the name of Thomas in to the Senate for confirmation as brigadier general. After he left the conference Sherman remembered that he had seen hardly anything of Thomas for twenty years and, a little anxious as to how he stood, he mounted his horse and rode out to the post in Maryland where Thomas was stationed. He found him in the saddle, and said to him, "Tom, you are a brigadier general." Thomas replied, "I don't know of any one that I would rather hear such news from than you." "But," said Sherman, "there are some stories about your loyalty. How are you going?" "Billy," answered Thomas, "I am going south!" "My God!" exclaimed Sherman, "Tom, you have put me in an awful position; I have become responsible for your loyalty." "Give yourself no trouble, Billy," said Thomas; "I am going south, but at the head of my men!" How Thomas kept his promise, let Mill Spring, Stone River, Chickamauga, Missionary Ridge, and Nashville answer. It was this loyal Virginian whose command saved the day at Stone River when McCook and Sheridan had been swept from the field; this same Virginian against whose lines in the solitudes of Chickamauga the whole Confederate army hurled itself only to be flung back like waves breaking on a rocky headland; it was the soldiers of Thomas who carried the rifle pits in their inspired charge up Missionary Ridge, and it was the army under his command which annihilated the army of Hood at Nashville. Had Sherman done nothing else during the war but secure the appointment to high rank of that noble and heroic character, his contribution to the success of the war would have been most notable. The fame of Thomas has not been commensurate with his distinguished service. But as time sifts the men and measures of our great struggle for national unity, the name of

Thomas, the Virginian who put his nation above his state, will grow in worthy fame and honorable renown.

At this interview at the *Willard* Sherman impressed upon Lincoln the fact that he did not wish to be left in a superior command, but was perfectly willing to serve in a subordinate capacity. Lincoln assured him there would be no difficulty about that, as his chief trouble was to find places for the generals who wished to command armies and be at the head of affairs. The worries and harassments incident to the setting up of a new department proved too trying for General Anderson, and early in October he was relieved of the command of the Department of the Cumberland and Sherman succeeded him. This introduced Sherman to the most painful chapter in his career. Most of the recruits which the loyal states had raised were streaming either into Washington, to McClellan's army, or in the direction of Fremont at St. Louis. Sherman's command received few troops, and as with keen military mind he realized his difficult position and the disproportion of the means at hand to the immensity of the task, he began to fret and complain, feeling that he was neglected by the Government. At his urgent request the Secretary of War, Simon Cameron, who had been to St. Louis to investigate Fremont's administration of affairs, on his way back to Washington stopped off for a day to visit Sherman at Louisville. He was accompanied by the adjutant-general of the army, Lorenzo Thomas. The conference was held in a room in the *Galt House.*

[104]

LINCOLN AND SHERMAN

Before taking up the discussions of his problems, Sherman asked for greater privacy, stating that many of those present were strangers to him. With some testiness of manner Cameron replied, "They are all friends, all members of my family, and you may speak your mind freely and without restraint." But among those present was a correspondent of the New York *Tribune,* and what Sherman supposed was a confidential and secret conversation was soon made public. During the interview, Cameron, who was unwell, lay on the bed. Sherman, in explaining to him the exigencies of the situation, said that he required 60,000 men for purposes of defense and 200,000 for offense. At this Cameron raised himself in the bed and exclaimed, "Great God! where are they to come from?" Convinced that he had at last aroused the Government to the seriousness of the situation in Kentucky and Tennessee, Sherman the next morning saw Cameron off for Washington.

When he reached Washington Cameron asked Adjutant-General Thomas to submit to him a memorandum of the events during his absence in the West. In this memorandum Thomas mentioned Sherman's "insane" request for 200,000 men. The newspapers at once took up the cry, and for several months Sherman was declared to be insane. Not long after he was relieved of his command and General Buell appointed to succeed him. This was in accordance with his understanding with the Government, but to the people at large it looked like a confirmation of the rumors of his insanity. He was transferred to Halleck's department at St.

Louis and did not see active duty in the field until the Shiloh campaign. Lincoln was in no way influenced by these newspaper slanders, and expressed his willingness to make Buell a major-general so that Sherman could serve under him and thus be retained in Kentucky. When Halleck sent Sherman home for a month's rest, he said in his explanation to General McClellan, "I am satisfied that General Sherman's physical and mental system is so completely broken by labor and care as to render him, for the present, unfit for duty; perhaps a few weeks' rest may restore him." The fact of the matter was that Sherman was in a nervous and irritable state of mind; but to say that he was insane, or in the least unbalanced, was a malicious slander.

Sherman's part in Shiloh, Vicksburg and Chattanooga made him one of the great personalities of the war. Yet during these years he had little contact or correspondence with Lincoln. When he was getting ready for his march from Chattanooga to Atlanta, Sherman commandeered all the rolling stock and foodstuffs in his neighborhood. This, of course, worked hardship upon the civilian population, and when complaint was made to Lincoln, who was always ready to listen to the voice of Union men in these Kentucky and Tennessee Mountains, he wrote to Sherman asking him if he could in some way modify his orders. Sherman refused to do so, telling the President that the railroad could not supply both the army and the people. "One or the other must quit, and the army don't intend to, unless Joe Johnston makes us."

LINCOLN AND SHERMAN

Lincoln made no further remonstrance and Sherman was left a free hand in his preparation for the great thrust into the heart of the Confederacy.

Sherman, like all men, had his peculiarities, and sometimes these peculiarities bordered on insubordination. In the midst of the Atlanta campaign he received notification from General James A. Hardie, the Inspector-General of the army, that Generals Osterhaus and Hovey, then serving under Sherman, had been made major-generals. Both of these men had gone to the rear, Osterhaus because of sickness and Hovey because of disagreement with General Schofield. Sherman was angry that these men had been elevated and other officers with him passed over, and telegraphed Hardie a message which concluded with these words: "If the rear be the post of honor, then we had better all change front on Washington." This dispatch was shown to the President, who, instead of resenting its unjust slur, wrote Sherman a kindly letter, expressing willingness to promote any officers whom Sherman might name and reminding him that in the cases of Osterhaus and Hovey the President had been chiefly influenced by the recommendations of Generals Grant and Sherman! The impetuous Sherman was, as he himself puts it, "fairly caught" for once, and telegraphed the President his apology, saying that he did not suppose such messages reached him personally, and that he had recommended Osterhaus and Hovey when the events of the Vicksburg campaign were fresh in his mind.

After the fall of Atlanta Sherman and Lincoln

attempted to supplement the military campaign by what in the World War would have been called "propaganda". There was perhaps no Southern state in which the feeling against Jefferson Davis was so strong as it was in Georgia, and Sherman and Lincoln tried to capitalize that feeling and thus withdraw Georgia from the war. Prominent Georgia citizens in conversation with Sherman had given expression to the futility of further resistance and expressed the wish that Governor Brown would withdraw the people of Georgia from the Confederacy. One of these men was commissioned to tell Governor Brown that if he would come and talk with Sherman he should have safe conduct and a respectful hearing. About this time Governor Brown had disbanded the Georgia militia and sent the members home to harvest the corn and sorghum of the state. For this action Brown was denounced as a traitor by Jefferson Davis. Lincoln evinced the keenest interest in these maneuvers of Sherman, and telegraphed him on September 17, 1864, "I feel great interest in the subject of your dispatch, mentioning corn and sorghum, and the contemplated visit to you." The same day Sherman telegraphed to Lincoln telling of his exchanges with Governor Brown and how he had said to the Governor's emissaries, "that some of the people of Georgia are engaged in rebellion, begun in error and perpetuated in pride, but that Georgia can now save herself from the devastations of war preparing for her, only by withdrawing her quota out of the Confederate army and aiding to expel Hood from the borders of the state; in which event, instead of desolating the land as we progress, I will keep our men to the high roads and commons, and pay for the corn and meat we need and take. I am fully conscious of the delicate nature of such assertions, but it would be a magnificent stroke of policy if we could, without surrendering principle or a foot of ground, arouse the latent enmity of Georgia against Davis." But the times proved not to be ripe for this stroke of policy, and Georgia was to feel once more the iron tread of Sherman's legions.

On the 12th of November, 1864, Sherman severed connections with his rear and set out on his famous march to the sea at Savannah. For a whole month there were no tidings from him, except the vague and alarming reports which came in by way of the Southern newspapers. During this period Lincoln was anxious, but confident. One day Colonel McClure of Pennsylvania called at the White House. As he was leaving Lincoln said, with a twinkle in his eye, "McClure, wouldn't you like to hear something from Sherman?" Everybody in the North just at that time was hoping to hear some word of Sherman and his army, and McClure responded, "Yes, most of all I should like to hear from Sherman." To this Lincoln answered, with a laugh, "Well, I'll be hanged if I wouldn't myself!"

When Sherman's brother John, calling at the White House, expressed anxiety about him and his army and asked Lincoln if he had heard any of the reports about Sherman having been outflanked and driven back, Lincoln said, "Oh, no. I know what hole he went in at, but I can't tell what hole he will come out of."

At length, on the 22nd of December, the message came to Lincoln telling of the capture of Savannah. In this message Sherman said, "I beg to present you as a Christmas gift the city of Savannah." In his acknowledgment of this splendid gift to the nation Lincoln wrote to Sherman:

My dear General Sherman:

Many, many thanks for your Christmas gift, the capture of Savannah. When you were about leaving Atlanta for the Atlantic coast I was anxious if not fearful; but feeling that you were the better judge, and remembering that "nothing risked, nothing gained," I did not interfere. Now, the undertaking being a success, the honor is all yours, for I believe none of us went farther than to acquiesce. And taking the work of General Thomas into the count, as it should be taken, it is, indeed, a great success. Not only does it afford the obvious and immediate military advantages, but in showing to the world that your army could be divided, putting the stronger part to an important new service, and yet leaving enough to vanquish the old opposing force of the whole— Hood's army—it brings those who sat in darkness to see a great light. But what next? I suppose it will be safe if I leave General Grant and yourself to decide. Please make my grateful acknowledgments to your whole army, officers and men.

The great career of Sherman as a commander in the Civil War came to an end in a bitter and unfortunate dispute with his Government. This was due to the repudiation of the terms of surrender of the Confederate army under General Joseph E. Johnston. Sherman maintained that in giving Johnston these terms he was following the wishes of Lincoln as indicated to him at a conference held at City Point. When his army was at Goldsboro, North Carolina, Sherman went to Grant's headquarters, City Point, on the James River, to confer with his commander-in-chief. At the same time Lincoln was there; also Admiral Porter. Sherman says that when he went on board the steamer *River Queen,* on which the President was living, Lincoln remembered him perfectly; but Admiral Porter, in his account of the interview, says that Lincoln did not remember having met Sherman before, until Sherman reminded him of the circumstances of their former meeting at Washington. Lincoln was much entertained by Sherman's stories of the exploits of his "bummers" and told other stories in return. The next day, March 28, 1865, Sherman again called on Lincoln on the *River Queen.* Grant and Porter were also present. Lincoln expressed great distress when Grant and Sherman told him that they thought another great battle would have to be fought before the war would come to an end. Sherman told him that the only ones who could prevent another great battle were the enemy. Sherman then asked Lincoln if all was ready for the end of the war. What was to be done with rebel armies when defeated; and with the political leaders? Lincoln said that all was ready; that all he wanted was to get the Confederate soldiers back on the farms and into the shops. As for Jefferson Davis, he illustrated his wish by telling one of his characteristic anecdotes about a total abstinence man who was invited by a friend to have a drink, but declined on the ground of his pledge. His friends suggested lemonade as an agreeable substitute. As he was preparing the lemonade the friend pointed to a bottle of brandy and said a few drops of the brandy would add greatly to the lemonade. His guest said that if the brandy were added "unbeknownst" to him, he would not object. It was thus plain that Lincoln hoped that Jefferson Davis would be permitted to flee the country. Lincoln also authorized Sherman to assure Governor Vance and the people of North Carolina that as soon as the rebel armies laid down their arms and resumed their civil pursuits, they would be guaranteed all their rights as citizens of a common country; and that to avoid anarchy the State governments then in existence, with their civil functionaries, would be recognized by him as the government *de facto* till Congress could provide others. Admiral Porter, who took notes during this interview, confirms the account given by Sherman.

When, therefore, on the 7th of April, Sherman met General Johnston at the Bennet house, near Durham, North Carolina, to arrange for the surrender of his army, there was no doubt in his mind as to what Lincoln desired and what he was authorized to arrange. On the way to the meeting he was handed the telegram telling of the assassination of the President. Sherman kept the news from his army, but showed the dispatch to Johnston when they met. The latter manifested the deepest distress, and the perspiration came out in large drops on his forehead. After the truce had been arranged for, Sherman and Johnston again met the next day. At this meeting Johnston was accompanied by General Breckenridge, the Secretary of War in Davis' cabinet. Johnston requested that he be permitted to sit, not as representative of the Confederate Government, but as a general in the army. To this Sherman assented. After proposed terms written by Postmaster-General Reagan of the Confederate cabinet had been read and rejected, Sherman, recalling what Lincoln had said to him at City Point, took up his pen and with an extraordinary facility which amazed Johnston, wrote off the draught of the terms which were finally adopted.

The terms concerning the officers and soldiers of Johnston's army were the same as those given by Grant to Lee the week before at Appomattox. The paragraphs which raised a storm at Washington and led to the repudiation of the whole agreement were those which provided for the storing of the arms of the Confederate soldiers in the State arsenals, the recognition of the State governments and a proclamation that the war was to cease followed by a general amnesty. The moment Grant read these terms he saw that they were impossible, and when he submitted them to the new President and the Secretary of War, a meeting of the Cabinet was immediately called and there was the greatest consternation lest Sherman should commit the Government to terms which it was not willing to grant. A foolish order was sent to the troops in the South not to obey Sherman, and Grant himself was sent to take charge of matters in South

Carolina. He discharged his difficult and delicate mission with the greatest tact, and Sherman, although deeply hurt and chagrined, notified Johnston that his terms had not been accepted by the Government of the United States and that, in forty-eight hours, according to the agreement of the truce, he would attack him. A new arrangement was then made with Johnston whereby he surrendered his army as Lee had done at Appomattox. The Government's rejection of Sherman's pact with Johnston was published, with the implied censure on Sherman, and worst of all the order of Halleck to Meade, commander of the Army of the Potomac, to march against Johnston and attack him regardless of Sherman's orders. This raised a great storm in the North, and Sherman, but yesterday the idolized hero of the war, became the most execrated man in the army. But this storm of national passion soon blew over, and the great soldier was restored to popular favor and to the admiration of the ages.

The mistake that Sherman made was to include political as well as military considerations in his terms with Johnston. Any one reading over the paragraphs of the agreement will be impressed with the fact that it was a treaty of peace rather than the surrender of a hostile army. The biographers of Lincoln asseverate that Sherman's presumption was due to the fact that he had a low opinion of all civilians and thought the generals in the field more competent to make war or peace than the politicians at Washington. This probably was true; but even with such views, Sherman

[114]

would not have ventured to propose such an instrument to Johnston unless he had felt that he was only putting into effect the desires of Lincoln as expressed to him at City Point. Some days before that meeting the Secretary of War had sent Grant a telegram telling him that it was the President's wish that he have no conferences with General Lee "unless it be for the capitulation of Lee's army or on solely minor or purely military matters. He instructs me to say that you are not to decide, discuss or confer upon any political question. Such questions the President holds in his own hands, and will submit them to no military conferences or conventions." If a copy of these orders of March 3rd had been sent to Sherman the whole difficulty might have been obviated; but this was not done, and even if it had been done, at the City Point conference, held ten days after hese orders were sent to Grant, Lincoln seemed to give Sherman authority to do just what he did in the first agreement with Johnston.

There are many conjectures as to what might have happened had Lincoln been spared and permitted to carry out his own policy of reconstruction, for it was contrary to the temper of the nation. The explosion of indignation which followed the publication of Sherman's terms with Johnston, which were a résumé of Lincoln's own policy of reconstruction, revealed all too plainly that the nation did not approve of Lincoln's clemency, and that even Lincoln himself, had he been spared, could never have secured for such a policy the ratification of the will of the people. Four years of suffering and distress had bred a different temper in the nation, and such a thing as the immediate recognition of the State governments, and the general amnesty, would have been impossible. Complete proof of this is shown by the fact that Lincoln himself had to withdraw the permission for the assembling of the Legislature of Virginia, and when he had formulated a message to Congress in February, 1865, proposing that $400,000,-000 be paid to the South as compensation for the emancipation of the slaves, it met with the unanimous disapproval of the Cabinet. We can only imagine what the nation would have thought had it known that such a thing had been proposed.

The half-century and more which has passed since the close of the Civil War has raised Abraham Lincoln to the rank of martyr, saint and prophet. But we must not read the thought and sentiments of the nation today into the mind of the nation of 1865. A general amnesty and the quick recognition of the States which had been in revolt against the Government appear at this day the natural and easy course to have been followed, all the more because we know it was the policy of Abraham Lincoln, the nation's great hero. But a nation is greater than its greatest man, and the accumulated indignation of the people would have swept Lincoln's overmild policy of reconstruction aside as surely as the wind drives the leaves before it.

LINCOLN AND BURNSIDE

General Ambrose E. Burnside was an officer who, both by his own confession and by the estimate of those associated with him, was not fitted for high command. Yet he had more independent commands and saw more fighting than almost any other general of the Civil War. Besides the command of the Army of the Potomac, Burnside led the expedition against the North Carolina forts in 1862, and, at the head of the Army of the Ohio, marched into eastern Tennessee in the campaign of Knoxville. From 1861 until July, 1864, when he was relieved by Grant after the Petersburg mine fiasco, Burnside was continually in the midst of stirring events, both as a soldier and as an administrator, for, as we shall see, his administration of the Department of the Ohio precipitated one of the most bitter political discussions of the war. Yet he was a man who had greatness thrust upon him. Thrice he was proffered by Lincoln the command of the Army of the Potomac, and twice he refused the great post, and when it was offered to him the third time he accepted it only with protests and tears. He sought to avoid the great honors and the great responsibilities of the conflict, but they gave him no rest.

In contrast with the aristocratic McClellan and Meade, both heirs of old Philadelphia culture and learning, Burnside was a child of the log cabin, born at Liberty, Indiana, on the 23rd of May, 1824.

The Mexican War was about over when he was graduated from West Point, and after six years in the army he resigned his commission and engaged in the manufacture of firearms in Rhode Island. When the Civil War broke out he was in the employ of the Illinois Central Railroad. It was in this service that he became intimate with McClellan. He commanded a Rhode Island brigade in the battle of Bull Run and early the next year led the very successful expeditionary force against the North Carolina coast. His successes there made him a major-general and his name well known to the public.

When McClellan's retreat down the Peninsula had shaken the President's confidence in him, Lincoln began to cast about for a new commander for the Army of the Potomac. The man he hit upon was Burnside, who peremptorily declined it. For the time being Lincoln had to be content with taking McClellan's army away from him instead of supplanting him with another commander. But the disaster of Second Bull Run made it necessary for Lincoln to recall McClellan to command the forces about Washington, disorganized by the defeat. Before restoring McClellan to command, Lincoln had a second time offered the post to Burnside, and again Burnside declined.

In the campaign which followed Burnside led his corps and did good service at South Mountain and Antietam, although his action at "Burnside" Bridge was slow and poorly executed. A few weeks later President Lincoln, exasperated by the

AMBROSE E. BURNSIDE

lack of progress McClellan was making in his movement against Lee, surprised the army and the entire country by placing Burnside in command. When word was brought to him at his headquarters at Orlean, Virginia, Burnside protested earnestly against taking the post, telling his staff that he did not regard himself competent to command so large an army. Yet he was a patriot, ready to serve where he was called, and although he did not think himself competent he knew of others whom he thought were even less fit, and lest they should be called if he refused, he accepted his new commission. It was a sad day for two men when, on that snowy 7th of November, 1862, Burnside walked into the tent of his friend and commander, McClellan, and showed him the President's order. With a smile McClellan accepted the inevitable and spent two days with Burnside helping him get hold of the situation. After Fitz John Porter, Burnside was perhaps McClellan's most intimate friend. Fond as he was of Burnside, McClellan knew too well that his coming to the command boded ill for the army. In his letter of that night to his wife, he said, "They have made a great mistake. Alas for my poor country!"

There was no question about the mistake that had been made. But how terrible a mistake it would prove to be, neither McClellan nor any other man could have foreseen. The bloody slopes of Fredericksburg, on the 13th of the following December, revealed how sad and tragic a mistake it was. The wonder is how Lincoln could ever have made it. Many of the generals whom Lincoln chose disappointed him and the whole country. But Burnside was Lincoln's one great military blunder. Fremont, Butler, Hooker, Pope, McClellan, Sigel— all made serious mistakes, and had characteristics which impaired their usefulness, but the blunder of Burnside was colossal. None of the high officials in the army had advocated Burnside as their partisans had advocated McClellan and Hooker. The man himself confessed that he was not equal to the task of leading the army to victory. Yet to him Lincoln gave the commander's baton. In this Lincoln must have been influenced by the personal charm and frank, open ways of Burnside. The idea of a dictator had been associated with McClellan, and when he determined to remove McClellan after Antietam Lincoln was evidently making sure of a general concerning whose complete separation from any political entanglement there could be no doubt. There was little likelihood of any factions or parties framing themselves about Burnside. He was too frank, too ingenuous, for that. He was popular with his men of the 9th Corps, but beyond this there was nothing in his military career thus far that singled him out as a leader of a great army.

McClellan had been relieved for moving too slowly and reluctantly. The new commander was expected to move against the enemy, and to move immediately. He did so. Burnside rejected the President's plan of campaign which had first been submitted to McClellan, and chose to cross the Rappahannock at Fredericksburg. But from the very beginning of the campaign things went wrong. The pontoons did not arrive as soon as expected, and one delay after another ensued, so that when Burnside finally got ready to move across the river, Lee's army was strongly established on the opposite heights. Burnside might have moved up or down the river, but he marched as the Israelites marched when they crossed the Jordan, "right against Jericho." He was expected to fight. Why not fight the enemy in the first place you find him? The crossing and the attack at Fredericksburg was commendable in its boldness and courage, but nothing more can be said of it. It was magnificent, but it was not war. Burnside wrote to Lincoln before the attack was made, "I think the enemy will be more surprised by a crossing immediately in our front than on any part of the river." They were surprised, but not taken by surprise. They were astounded by the frontal assault, but not dumbfounded by it. As one of Burnside's West Point friends in the Confederate army said to him during the truce, "We thought you had more sense than to batter your brains out against our stone walls." After the battle, Burnside, standing at his headquarters at Falmouth, and pointing to the thousands of dead and dying men lying on the field across the river, groaned aloud to General W. F. Smith, "Oh, those men! Oh, those men over there!" And the whole nation, when it heard the story, echoed the cry, "Oh, those men! Oh, those men over there!"

The extraordinary thing is that the disaster at Fredericksburg did nothing to change or weaken the popular estimate of Burnside. In his own army there was lack of confidence and bitter criticism, but outside, no clamor and tumults were raised as happened after other reverses.

This retention by Burnside of the nation's confidence, and Lincoln's too, was due in large part to the manly way in which he assumed the entire responsibility for what had taken place. In his report to General Halleck, Burnside said, "To the brave officers and men who accomplished the feat of this recrossing in the face of the enemy, I owe everything. For the failure in the attack I am responsible, as the extreme gallantry, courage and endurance shown by them was never excelled, and would have carried the points, had it been possible. The fact that I decided to move from Warrenton on this line rather against the opinion of the President, Secretary, and yourself, and that you have left the whole management in my hands, without giving me orders, makes me the more responsible."

In reply to this report Lincoln, fearing that the soldiers would be greatly depressed over the recent defeat, addressed a special message to the Army of the Potomac. In this message Lincoln said: "Although you were not successful, the attempt was not an error, nor the failure other than an accident. The courage with which you, in an open field, maintained the contest against an intrenched foe, and the consummate skill and success with which you crossed and recrossed the river in the face of the enemy, show that you possess all the qualities of a great army, which will yet give victory to the cause of the country and of popular government. Condoling with the mourners for the dead and sympathizing with the severely wounded, I congratulate you that the number of both is comparatively small. I tender you, officers and soldiers, the thanks of the nation."

Burnside made two more attempts to cross the river. The first was stopped by orders from Lincoln and the second by the mud. When Burnside was preparing for his new effort to cross the river Lincoln wrote a letter to Halleck asking him to direct and advise Burnside. Few letters of Lincoln's show such distress and reveal such a sense of inability to direct the military operations. In it Lincoln said, "If in such a difficulty as this you do not help me, you fail me precisely in the point for which I sought your assistance. Tell General Burnside that you do approve or you do not approve his plan."

On the first day of January, 1863, Burnside, who was then contemplating a new movement against Lee's army, wrote of his plan to the President. In the letter he tells Lincoln that both Stanton and Halleck have not the confidence of the army and intimates that both of them must be removed if the army is to gain a victory. He then goes on to state how all his division commanders are opposed to his contemplated move and lack confidence in his leadership. He states it as his opinion that the army should be commanded by another officer who shall have the confidence of the under officers, and offers to make the way easy for the appointment of a successor by resigning his post. On the 5th day of January, Burnside, in a formal manner, tendered his resignation. Still Lincoln did not accept it. Here is a strange case. A general who confesses that he does not hold the confidence of his officers and asks to be relieved, yet is continued in power. Lincoln's dilemma was the nation's dilemma—Whom shall I have for a commander?

On the 23rd day of January Burnside telegraphed to Lincoln asking if he could see him after midnight that night, saying that he was preparing some very important orders which he would like to submit to the President. These were the famous General Orders, No. 8, in which Burnside dismisses Hooker from the army as a man unfit to hold an important commission. Other officers to be dismissed or relieved from duty with the army were Brooks, Newton, Cochrane, Franklin, W. F. Smith, and Sturgis. At the midnight interview Burnside submitted these preposterous orders to Lincoln for his approval, with the alternative of accepting his resignation. Lincoln, of course, chose the latter, and Hooker succeeded the frank and manly and patriotic Burnside.

The next chapter in Lincoln's relationships with Burnside contains one of the most stirring political incidents of the entire war. In March, 1863, Lincoln made Burnside commander of the Department of the Ohio, with headquarters at Cincinnati. He found that part of Ohio and the adjoining territory infested with bitter hostility to the Government, and with a commendable zeal Burnside determined to suppress its manifestations. To this end he issued the celebrated Order No. 38, in which he said that "all persons found within our

lines who commit acts for the benefit of the enemies of our country, will be tried as spies or
traitors, and, if convicted, will suffer death." The
order concluded with this statement, "It must be
distinctly understood that treason, expressed or
implied, will not be tolerated in this department."
Many of the friends of the administration thought
the order impolitic, and among the opposition it
aroused furious denunciation. The most bitter
and most eloquent assailant was Clement L. Vallandigham. Vallandigham had been a member of
Congress until his attacks on the Government lost
him his seat. In a speech in Congress in January,
1863, he said, "I did not support the war; and today I bless God that not the smell of so much as
one drop of its blood is upon my garments. Our
Southern brethren were to be whipped back into
love and fellowship at the point of the bayonet.
Oh, monstrous delusion! Sir, History will record
that, after nearly six thousand years of folly and
wickedness in every form of government, theo-
cratic, democratic, monarchic, oligarchic, despotic,
and mixed, it was reserved to American statesman-
ship, in the nineteenth century of the Christian era,
to try the grand experiment, on a scale the most
costly and gigantic in its proportions, of creating
love by force, and developing fraternal affection by
war; and History will record too, on the same
page, the utter, disastrous and most bloody failure
of the experiment." This was a sample of the powerful eloquence of this dangerous demagogue.

An army officer in citizen's clothes who attended
a mass meeting at Mt. Vernon, Ohio, heard Val-

landigham deliver a speech in which he bitterly denounced the Government, called Lincoln a tyrant, and said that Burnside's Order, No. 38, he despised, spat upon and trampled under his feet. This was too much for the patriotic Burnside who, as an army leader, had seen too many die in battle to be able to tolerate such utterances. A squad of soldiers arrested Vallandigham in his home at Dayton and took him to Cincinnati, where, in due course, he was tried by a military commission and found guilty of violating General Order, No. 38, by declaring disloyal sentiments and opinions, with the object and purpose of weakening the powers of the Government in its efforts to suppress an unlawful rebellion. He was sentenced to close confinement in a military fortress and General Burnside ordered him sent to Fort Warren, Boston.

Lincoln was disturbed and embarrassed by the arrest of Vallandigham. Had he been consulted beforehand it would not have taken place. But now that Burnside had taken the stand and that the passions of the nation had been aroused on one side or the other, Lincoln could do nothing but stand by Burnside. But he relieved the tension somewhat and injected an element of humor into the whole matter by taking advantage of one of the clauses of Burnside's order, in which he said that those found guilty of expressing sympathy for the enemy would be "sent beyond our lines into the lines of their friends." The sentence of Vallandigham was commuted to expulsion from the Union lines, and he was unceremoniously dumped between the lines of the armies of Rosecrans and

Bragg, then confronting one another near Murfreesboro in Tennessee. After a brief stay in the South,
Vallandigham ran the blockade and went to Bermuda and thence to Canada. From the Canadian
side he issued an address to the people of Ohio,
where the Democrats had nominated him for Governor, in which he said, "Arrested and confined for
three weeks in the United States a prisoner of
state; banished thence to the Confederate States,
I found myself first a freeman when on British soil.
And today, under the protection of the British flag,
I am here to enjoy and, in part, to exercise the
privileges and rights which usurpers insolently
deny me at home."

The arrest of Vallandigham was more bitterly
criticized and disputed than any act of the Government during the war. All those opposed to the
administration rallied round the incident and began
to make use of it for political purposes. On the
16th of May, 1863, a public meeting of protest was
held at Albany, New York. In a message to the
meeting Governor Seymour of New York wrote:
"It is an act which has brought dishonor upon our
country. If it is upheld our liberties are over-
thrown. The action of the administration will determine, in the minds of more than one-half of the
people of the loyal states, whether this war is
waged to put down rebellion in the South, or to
destroy free institutions at home." The meeting
adopted resolutions of a similar tone to reverse
the action of Burnside's tribunal and set Vallandigham free.

LINCOLN AND HIS GENERALS

To these resolutions Lincoln answered in one of his longest and most carefully considered papers, defending the right of the Government to act as it had in the case of Vallandigham. As for the menace to civil liberty and constitutional rights, he said the act was an extraordinary act for an extraordinary crisis; that even in times of peace "bands of horse thieves and robbers frequently grow too numerous and powerful for the ordinary courts of justice. But what comparison in numbers have such bands ever borne to the insurgent sympathizers, even in many of the loyal states? Again, a jury too frequently has at least one member more ready to hang the panel than to hang the traitor. And, yet again, he who dissuades one man from volunteering, or induces one soldier to desert, weakens the Union cause as much as he who kills a Union soldier in battle." Referring to the alleged danger of civil procedure being supplanted by acts of military courts, Lincoln pointedly and humorously said: "Nor am I able to appreciate the danger apprehended by the meeting that the American people will, by means of military arrests during the rebellion, lose the right of public discussion, the liberty of speech and the press, the law of evidence, trial by jury, and habeas corpus, throughout the indefinite peaceful future which I trust lies before them, any more than I am able to believe that a man could contract so strong an appetite for emetics, during temporary illness, as to persist in feeding upon them during the remainder of his healthful life." In a more serious vein the President spoke of how men like Vallandigham, by their speeches, encouraged desertion in the army. "Long experience has shown that armies cannot be maintained unless desertion shall be punished by the severe penalty of death. The case requires, and the law and the constitution sanction, this punishment. Must I shoot a simple-minded soldier boy who deserts, while I must not touch a hair of a wily agitator who induces him to desert? This is none the less injurious when effected by getting a father, or brother, or friend into a public meeting and there working upon his feelings till he is persuaded to write the soldier boy that he is fighting in a bad cause, for a wicked administration of a contemptible Government, too weak to arrest and punish him if he shall desert. I think that in such a case to silence the agitator and save the boy is not only constitutional, but, withal, a great mercy." There was Lincoln at his best.

Vallandigham, overwhelmingly defeated in the Ohio elections, defied the order of expulsion and returned to the United States in June, 1864, where he delivered speeches more violent and bitter than those for which he had been deported. But Lincoln wisely refused to pay any attention to him. Vallandigham's last act of political importance was the part he took in the Chicago Convention which nominated McClellan for the presidency and declared the war to be a failure. His dramatic career was cut short by an accident in the year 1871. He was chief counsel for the defense in a murder trial at Lebanon, Ohio, and was demonstrating to some of his associate counsel in his room at the hotel, the impossibility of the accused having fired the fatal shot. There were two pistols on the table, and to illustrate his argument Vallandigham took up one of the pistols and holding it to his head in the place where the bullet had entered the dead man's head, pulled the trigger. By mistake he had taken up the loaded pistol and fell mortally wounded and shortly afterwards expired. The son of a Presbyterian minister, he was expelled from Jefferson College as a lad, and his whole career was full of dramatic episodes, not one of the least of which was the part he took in interrogating John Brown when he lay wounded on the floor of the engine house at Harper's Ferry in 1859.

During the campaign of Rosecrans against Bragg in eastern Tennessee, Burnside conducted an army to Knoxville. After the disaster which befell the Union army at Chickamauga, when it was compelled to fall back into Chattanooga, Longstreet was detached from Bragg's army and moved against Burnside, besieging him at Knoxville. The greatest apprehension was felt by the Government for the safety of Burnside and his army, and the first thing Grant did after crushing Bragg in the battle of Chattanooga, was to send Sherman to the relief of Burnside. But Burnside had conducted affairs with great courage and skill, and had successfully withstood Longstreet long before Sherman appeared. General Foster had been sent to relieve Burnside at his own request, and when as far as Cumberland Gap, reported that he could get little news of Burnside and the siege of Knoxville, except that his scouts reported heavy firing in that direction. It was when he had received one of these messages after a day of anxiety, that Lincoln expressed his confidence and satisfaction as to Burnside's position by the following bit of anecdotage: "A neighbor of mine in Menard County, named Sally Ward, had a large family of children that she took very little care of. Whenever she heard one of them yelling in some out-of-the-way place she would say, 'Thank the Lord! there's one of my young ones not dead yet!'" The reports of heavy firing in the direction of Knoxville let Lincoln know that one of his generals was not yet captured.

Upon being relieved from the command of the Department of the Ohio, Burnside went back to his old Corps, the 9th, and led it gallantly through the heavy fighting of the Wilderness under Grant. His long career in the army came to an abrupt and unfortunate conclusion after the failure of the Petersburg Mine attack.

When the army was before Petersburg Burnside's Ninth Corps had fought its way to within one hundred and thirty yards of the Confederate position. An officer in one of Burnside's divisions, who had been a mine expert in the anthracite regions of Pennsylvania, suggested to Burnside that a mine be dug under the Confederate lines. The men, many of whom had been miners, entered into the project with the greatest industry and enthusiasm. The main gallery was 510 feet in length, with two lateral galleries thrust under the fort. Three hundred and twenty kegs of powder were stowed away in the eight magazines. The explosion was set for the 30th of July. Wild rumors were abroad in the Confederate lines as to the mine, and their troops were filled with apprehension and unrest. Finally, at five o'clock in the morning, after the first fuse had burned out, the mine exploded, tearing a great chasm in the earth and carrying terror to the heart of the enemy. Burnside had carefully drilled a division of colored troops for the assault, but at the last moment a white division was substituted. There was bad behavior on the part of some of the officers, and the troops, poorly led, pressed down into the crater and were soon in seething and hopeless disorder. To add to the confusion and debacle the division of colored troops was ordered up. The negroes fought with the greatest gallantry, but they had come too late and were soon thrust back by the reorganized Confederates into the inferno at the bottom of the crater. The vast pit was now filled with a struggling mass of white and colored troops, cowering against the steep sides and vainly seeking shelter from the fire of the Confederate artillery. The blood of men wounded near the top of the crater flowed in streams down the yellow sides of the crater, and gathered into pools at the bottom. Men who had been shot at the top came rolling down the steep sides, or ran screaming and cursing through the mob. The sun, now high in heaven, aggravated the sufferings of the victims in the crater, and a wave of moisture produced by the breathing of the bloody, struggling, perspiring mass, rose like a cloud over the scene of horror. Thrown into this terrible pit by the blunders of their officers, the men were left in the crater for hour after hour, without orders, and it was not until two in the afternoon that two of the brigadiers with the troops, gave, on their own responsibility, the order to retire. The Petersburg crater was one of the ghastliest tragedies of the war, and once again it was Burnside who was immediately responsible for the blunder. The two division commanders, it was discovered, had been crouching like cowards in their bomb-proof shelters while their men, waiting in vain for orders, were left struggling in the shambles at the bottom of the crater. The only redeeming feature of the whole ghastly action was the magnificent conduct of the black troops.

Both Grant and Meade blamed Burnside for the disaster. The Court of Inquiry, ordered by the President at the request of Meade, censured Burnside for neglecting the preparations necessary to insure success, but the Committee on the Conduct of the War justified Burnside in every particular and laid the responsibility for the failure at the door of Meade and Grant. From the evidence at hand it seems clear that if Burnside's carefully trained negro troops had been permitted to take the part which Burnside had intended them to take, the chances of success would have been much greater.

Burnsides' resignation never would have been accepted by Lincoln until the war was over. But it arrived on the day of his assassination, and one of the first official acts of President Johnson was its acceptance. Thus, with the fall of his great chief, the noble-minded, magnanimous patriot, Burnside, passed into civil life. He left behind him a record of unblemished character and high fearlessness. His service was long and many of his achievements notable. But he will be remembered for the great and tragic mistake of Fredericksburg. When we think of Burnside, we see a haggard general pointing across the Rappahannock to where thousands of his soldiers lay dead and dying on the bloody slopes of Marye Heights, and groaning aloud to the members of his staff who stood near him, "Oh, those men! Oh, those men over there!"

LINCOLN AND HOOKER

"General Joseph Hooker, having been guilty of unjust and unnecessary criticism of the actions of his superior officers, and of the authorities, and having by the general tone of his conversation endeavored to create distrust in the minds of officers who have associated with him, and for habitually speaking in disparaging terms of other officers, is hereby dismissed the service of the United States as a man unfit to hold an important commission during a crisis like the present, when so much patience, charity, confidence, consideration, and patriotism are due from every soldier in the field. This order is issued subject to the approval of the President of the United States."

So ran the extraordinary order which General A. E. Burnside, Commander of the Army of the Potomac, submitted to President Lincoln a few weeks after the disastrous repulse of the army before the heights of Fredericksburg. Lincoln did not approve the order, and the next day, January 25, 1863, appointed to the command of the Army of the Potomac, General Joseph Hooker, described by Burnside as "a man unfit to hold an important commission during a crisis like the present." In making this appointment Lincoln consulted none of his colleagues. He had, indeed, in the previous summer, about the time of the battle of Second Bull Run, said to his Secretary of the Navy, Gideon Welles, "Who can take command of this army?

Who is there among all the generals?" Without much consideration Welles named Hooker. Lincoln replied, "I think as much as you or any other man of Hooker, but I fear he gets excited." Postmaster-General Blair, who was present, said he thought Hooker was too great a friend of John Barleycorn, whereupon Welles answered, "If his habits are bad, if he ever permits himself to get intoxicated, he ought not to be trusted with such a command." This lets us know that long before he was made commander of the army Hooker was highly thought of by those in authority at Washington. But when he appointed him to that post Lincoln acted by himself and for himself.

Joseph Hooker was born on the 13th of November, 1813, at Hadley, Massachusetts. He was graduated from West Point in 1837, and served with distinction in the Mexican War. After a few years' service as assistant adjutant-general in California, where he was intimate with Grant, Sherman, and Halleck, Hooker purchased a tract of land in Sonoma County, California, and tried his hand, but with indifferent success, at ranching. In anticipation of the war between the States, Hooker had become the colonel of a California regiment of infantry. When the war broke out he had not sufficient funds to get to the scene of hostilities, and generous and admiring friends raised a sum of one thousand dollars to defray his traveling expenses. No attention was paid to his application for a commission in the army by the authorities at Washington, probably due to the fact that testy old General Scott, then in command, had not forgot-

JOSEPH HOOKER

ten how the impudent young artillery officer had criticized him during the Mexican War. Shortly after the Battle of Bull Run, which he had witnessed as a mere spectator, Hooker, about to go back in chagrin to California, was presented to Lincoln at the White House. The friend who introduced him named him as "Captain" Hooker. Hooker then said to the President, "Mr. President, I am not 'Captain' Hooker, but was once Lieutenant-colonel Hooker, of the regular army. I was lately a farmer in California, but since the Rebellion broke out I have been here trying to get into the service, and I find that I am not wanted. I am about to return home, but before going I was anxious to pay my respects to you, and to express my wishes for your personal welfare and success in quelling this Rebellion. And I want to say one word more. I was at Bull Run the other day, Mr. President, and it is no vanity in me to say that I am a damned sight better general than any you had on that field."

Such was the first meeting between Lincoln and the general who was in the next few years to arouse in Lincoln such high hopes, only to be dashed in dark disappointment. Shortly after this meeting Lincoln made Hooker a brigadier-general of volunteers. There must have been something in common between these two men, recognized by the acute Lincoln at the very first encounter, for Lincoln was more intimate with Hooker, talked with him more, than with any other commander of the Army of the Potomac. His messages to him were couched in a familiar and fatherly style, and the President, in his conversations and communications with Hooker, fell back easily and naturally into the vernacularities and jocosities of the West.

Hooker was regarded as the best-looking man in the Federal army. He was tall and well proportioned, his complexion as ruddy as a schoolgirl's, his hair a light brown. Some of his critics claim to have noted a weak chin in his make-up, but that probably was after Chancellorsville, and not before it. His best portraits show not only a good-looking man, but a face of high intelligence. His reputation for good looks was of long standing, for the ladies of Mexico City called him "El Capitan Hermoso," the handsome captain, and also applied to him an expression which meant "the only man as handsome as a woman." When mounted on his white charger Hooker presented a magnificent appearance, and his presence among his troops, in the midst of battle, never failed to evoke wild cheering.

In the Peninsular campaign Hooker led his corps with courage and skill, and he was soon one of the outstanding officers of the Army of the Potomac. The sobriquet by which he was known, "Fighting Joe," was not bestowed upon him by the troops, but by some nameless clerk of the Associated Press, who, when the reports of the Battle of Malvern Hill were coming in, put as a running head for one of the copy sheets the words "Fighting Joe Hooker." The newspapers ran the words at the head of their columns the next day and the sobriquet became inexorably linked with Hooker's career. It did not do him justice, for Hooker, although full of dash and fight when going into action, did not assault in mad frenzy nor without careful consideration of the end in view. It was this "Fighting Joe" Hooker, who, as commander of one of the Grand Divisions at Fredericksburg, rode to Burnside's headquarters and earnestly protested against the order to move his troops against the fatal heights of the Marye Mansion. The title was very distasteful to Hooker. "It always sounds to me," said Hooker, "as if it meant 'Fighting Fool'. It has really done me much injury in making the public believe I am a furious, headstrong fool, bent on making furious dashes at the enemy. I have never fought without good purpose and with fair chances of success. When I have decided to fight, I have done so with all the vigor and strength I could command."

After Malvern Hill it was Hooker who urged McClellan to move on Richmond, telling him that he might as well be hung for a lion as for an old sheep, meaning probably that he might as well risk his command of the army in a great forward movement against the capital of the Confederacy as lose it by inaction and the wrangling of politicians. At South Mountain and Antietam Hooker was in the thick of the fighting and was severely wounded in the latter conflict. His chief fault was unsparing criticism of his fellow-officers and even of his superiors. During the hearing of the dispute between Generals Pillow and Worth, about the storming of Chaupultepec, Hooker spoke severely of some of Scott's plans of assault and showed how he could have secured the same end with less cost of life. This, as we have seen, the vain old hero never forgot, and it almost cost Hooker a commission in the army. In his report of Fredericksburg he sarcastically concluded by saying that when he had lost all the men his orders required him to lose he withdrew his division from the fight. His criticisms must have been unusually bitter at this time, for Burnside's famous Order No. 8 dismissing Hooker from the army and excoriating him for his faults, indicates extraordinary provocation. Hooker never knew of this order and what Burnside had said of him until the campaign which culminated at Gettysburg was about to open. But when he did see it he expressed himself to Stanton in these violent words: "I see that Burnside's stupid Order No. 8 has at last found its way into the newspapers. It causes me no regret, and would no one else if the character of the author was as well understood by them as myself. His moral degradation is unfathomable. It has, and still grieves me to reflect that my surroundings at this time are such that I cannot call him to account for his atrocities and make him swallow his words, or face the music, before going into another fight. He must swallow his words as soon as I am in a condition to address him, or I will hunt him to the ends of the earth." We have no record that Hooker and Burnside ever met again.

Towards McClellan, Hooker was equally unsparing in his censure. He testified before the Committee of Congress to Investigate the War that the Peninsular campaign was lost because of "want of generalship on the part of the commander-in-chief."

LINCOLN AND HOOKER

In a message to Lincoln, after Chancellorsville, Hooker concluded, saying, "Jackson is dead, and Lee beats McClellan in his untruthful bulletins."

These characteristics of Hooker were by this time well known to Lincoln, for even the President had not been spared Hooker's energetic language. Lincoln refers to this in the fatherly letter which he sent Hooker when he made him commander of the army. No commander of an army ever received from the head of the State such a letter. The letter, which shows Lincoln at his best, ran as follows:

General: I have placed you at the head of the Army of the Potomac. Of course I have done this upon what appear to me sufficient reasons, and yet I think it is best for you to know that there are some things in regard to which I am not quite satisfied with you. I believe you to be a brave and skilful soldier, which, of course, I like. I also believe you do not mix politics with your profession, in which you are right. You have confidence in yourself, which is a valuable if not an indispensable quality. You are ambitious, which, within reasonable bounds, does good rather than harm; but I think that during General Burnside's command of the Army you have taken counsel of your ambition and thwarted him as much as you could, in which you did a great wrong to the country and to a most meritorious and honorable brother officer. I have heard, in such a way as to believe it, of your recently saying that both the army and the government needed a dictator. Of course, it was not for this, but in spite of this, that I have given you the command. Only those generals who gain successes can set up as dictators. What I now ask of you is military success, and I will risk the dictatorship. The government will support you to the utmost of its ability, which is neither more nor less than it has done and will do for all its commanders. I much fear that the spirit which you have aided to infuse into the army, of criticizing their commander and withholding confidence from him, will now turn upon you. I shall assist you as far as I can to put it down. Neither you nor Napoleon, if he were alive again, could get any good out of an army while such a spirit prevails in it. And now beware of rashness. Beware of rashness, but with energy and sleepless vigilance go forward and give us victories.

In this letter there is a mingling of that humor, pathos, and magnificent faith in the nation and its cause which are now forever associated with the name of Abraham Lincoln. When he tells Hooker that only successful generals can set up as dictators, the playful intimation is that the past history of the army has not led the President to have very strong misgivings as to the danger of a dictatorship. Together with this is the sorrow of Lincoln that Hooker and other of his generals should let their ambitions and personal prejudices stand in the way of that co-operation which is necessary to victory. Lincoln believed that McClellan and his generals had behaved badly at the time of the second battle of Bull Run and that their lack of cordial support cost Pope the victory and almost brought disaster to the nation. Yet he restored McClellan to the command. Here again he believed that Burnside's indictment of Hooker, as contained in the rejected Order No. 8, was on the whole true, and that Hooker had let his own ambitions stand in the way of loyal and prompt obedience, and that Burnside's ill success was due in part to Hooker. With appalling frankness Lincoln says this to Hooker, yet he gave him the command of the army beneath whose banners rested the hopes of the republic, for, as in the case of McClellan in the Antietam campaign, Lincoln hoped that Hooker, in spite of his faults, would give the country what it was praying for—victory.

Two others of the chief actors in the drama of the Civil War noted in Hooker this trait of ambition. Neither Grant nor Sherman liked Hooker, and their judgments are to be taken with that in mind. Yet Grant, at least, was generally fair and just in his comments upon the officers with whom he came in contact during the war. This is what he had to say of Hooker, who served under him in the November campaign of 1863, when, in the battle about Chattanooga, Grant defeated Bragg and relieved the nation from a great fear: "Of Hooker I saw but little during the war. I had known him very well before, however. Where I did see him, at Chattanooga, his achievement in bringing his command around the point of Lookout Mountain and into Chattanooga Valley was brilliant. I nevertheless regarded him as a dangerous man. He was not subordinate to his superiors. He was ambitious to the extent of caring nothing for the rights of others. His disposition was, when engaged in battle, to get detached from the main body of the army and exercise a separate command, gathering to his standard all he could of his juniors."

Sherman pays tribute to Hooker's dash as a fighter and complimented him for special gallantry at Peach Tree Creek. Yet he, too, mentions "this tendency to get detached from the main body of the army," and says that Thomas, McPherson and Schofield had all complained to him of this tendency to "switch off, leaving wide gaps in his line, so as to be independent, and to make glory on his own account." This habit, on one occasion, evoked a sharp reprimand from Sherman and was the chief reason why, when McPherson was killed in battle, Howard, instead of Hooker, was appointed to the command of the Army of the Tennessee.

The President's letter, as might have been expected from its tone, touched rather than irritated Hooker, who said of it, "He talks to me like a father. I shall not answer this letter until I have won him a great victory." The letter was never answered. With the rank and the file of the army Hooker's appointment to command was well received. But the majority of the superior officers were far from enthusiastic. Their attitude is reflected in the statement made long after the war by Major-General Darius N. Couch: "When Hooker, on January 25th, was placed in command of the army many of us were very much surprised. I think the superior officers did not regard him competent for the task. He had fine qualities as an officer, but not the weight of character to take charge of that army."

Hooker had often been mentioned as a brilliant and hard fighting corps commander. As the commander of an army in battle his associates did not rate him highly. But his fitness for the one thing that the Army of the Potomac then needed above all else, reorganization and the restoration of fighting spirit, does not seem to have been discussed by either the officials of the government or the officers of the army. Yet it was here, in this work of reorganization, of putting a spirit of confidence and daring into the army, that the great ability of Hooker first shone forth. In the very passage where he gives so unfavorable an opinion of Hooker, Couch generously acknowledges the miracle of reorganization accomplished by Hooker: "Nevertheless, under his administration the army was wonderfully vigorous. I have never known men to change from a condition of the lowest depression to that of a healthy fighting state in so short a time."

Never in all its history was the Army of the Potomac in such bad shape as it was in after Burnside's failures at Fredericksburg. The feat of General McClellan in the previous September, taking the army in hand and reorganizing it as he marched after Lee, was a military achievement of the highest order. But what McClellan had to contend with chiefly was the dislocation of the army, its regiments and divisions scattered about here and there. Hooker succeeded to the command of a compact army, yet his work of reorganization was a far greater one than that of McClellan on the way to Antietam, for the army which he took over from Burnside was dispirited and sulky. The men felt that they had been mishandled by incompetent leaders. Thousands of officers and men were away from the army on one kind of leave or another. Hundreds of men were deserting every day, and a spirit of cynicism and indifference was rife in the camps. One of the best New England regiments openly hurrahed for "Jeff" Davis when a Union officer of high rank rode by with his staff. This was the host that Hooker took and transformed into the army that shattered Lee at Gettysburg, for that battle, let it not be forgotten, came at the end of a campaign which was planned and executed by Hooker.

Among the features of Hooker's reorganization was the adoption of a corps badge, at once very popular with the soldiers. As for the deserters, Hooker secured greater liberty in dealing with them from the President, and a few shootings of deserters in the presence of the army had a very salutary effect. It was after Hooker took hold of the army that the cavalry of the Army of the Potomac began to count. Hooker organized them as a separate unit and the cavalry division steadily increased in spirit and fighting power, splendidly manifested in the Gettysburg campaign. The saying, "Who ever saw a dead cavalryman?" was one of the many attributed to Hooker. He did not use this expression as a slight upon that branch of the service, but he did announce his intention to make greater use of the cavalry, saying to one of his officers that he had not seen many dead cavalrymen lying about as yet, but that ere long there would be such a sight. In conversation with one of his cavalry brigadiers Hooker spoke of the superiority of the Northern trooper over his Southern adversary in point of food, mount and equipment, and he added, "Now, with such soldiers and such a cause as we have behind them—the best cause since the world began—we ought to be invincible, and by —, sir, we shall be! You have got to stop these disgraceful cavalry 'surprises'. I'll have no more of them. I give you full power over your officers, to arrest, cashier, shoot—whatever you will—only you must stop these 'surprises'. And, by —, sir, if you don't do it, I give you fair notice, I will relieve the whole of you, and take the command of the cavalry myself!"

By the first of April it was a different host which Hooker commanded on the heights opposite Fredericksburg, an army well drilled, thoroughly disciplined and full of fight, breaking out into wild cheering whenever their handsome general rode down the line, or singing as they marched for the fords of the Rappahannock,

"The Union boys are moving on the left and on the right,
 The bugle call is sounding, our shelters we must strike;
 Joe Hooker is our leader, he takes his whisky strong,
 So our knapsacks we will sling, and go marching along."

In the first week in April, Lincoln, accompanied by Mrs. Lincoln and "Tad," paid a visit to the army. The President, mounted on a black horse, his long legs nearly touching the ground, received a great ovation from the troops as he reviewed them, with the magnificent Hooker seated on a white horse at his side. He was greatly impressed with the miracle of the army reorganization and had every reason to think that he had not erred in placing Hooker at its head. Yet he had some misgivings, for Noah Brooks, who was with him on this visit, recalls how, after hearing Hooker talk

[147]

about the "finest army on the planet," and the oft-reiterated "When I take Richmond," Lincoln said confidentially to him, "This is the most depressing thing about Hooker. It seems to me that he is overconfident." At the close of a dinner party at headquarters Lincoln took Hooker and Couch aside and said to them, in words which were strangely prophetic of what caused the defeat in the coming battle, "Gentlemen, in your next battle, put in all your men." "Yet," as Couch significantly adds, "that is exactly what we did not do at Chancellorsville."

It was on this visit to the army that Lincoln talked with General Averell about the recent fight at Kepp's Ford with the Confederate cavalry under General Fitzhugh Lee. An incident of this fight was a rather unusual exchange of letters between Lee and Averell, who had been classmates at West Point, Lee advising Averell to leave Virginia and go home, or, failing that, to bring him, the next time he crossed the river, a sack of coffee. When he withdrew after the fight at Kepp's Ford, Averell left two men too severely wounded to be removed. To a surgeon remaining with the wounded men he gave a sack of coffee, with the following note to Lee:

Dear Fitz: Here's your coffee. Here's your visit. How do you like it?   Averell.

Lincoln carried the correspondence with him and would frequently produce and show it. He said to Averell:

"Were you and General Lee friends?"

"Certainly," said Averell, "and always have been."

"What would happen should you meet on the battlefield?"

"One or both of us would be badly hurt or killed."

At this Lincoln exclaimed, more to himself than to the bystanders:

"Oh, my God, what a dreadful thing is a war like this, in which personal friends must slay each other and die like fiends!"

In the last days of April, 1863, Hooker commenced the movement which culminated in the Battle of Chancellorsville. He had conceived what all students of war concede to have been a brilliant piece of strategy. The plan was so clear cut, with all its different movements climaxing in the blow which was to give victory to the Federal army, that it is a delight even to read an account of it. In brief it was this: The two armies lay facing one another at Fredericksburg with the Rappahannock River flowing between them. Hooker's plan was to have a large division of cavalry under General Stoneman cross the river at a point west of the Confederate army and then swing far into the rear of that army, cutting Lee's communications with Richmond and threatening that city. As soon as that movement was well under way the main portion of the Army of the Potomac was to cross the river to the northwest of the Confederate army, getting into its immediate rear and advance towards it, while the troops left at Fredericksburg crossed at that point and marched on the foe. With his line of communications endangered by the cavalry raid towards Richmond and with two Union armies marching against him, one on his rear and another on his front, Lee's army would be crushed or compelled to make a dangerous retreat on Richmond.

The raid of the cavalry did not accomplish what Hooker expected of it, but the general movement of the army was a great success. Without opposition from the enemy, Hooker succeeded in transporting the army over the river and had it well established in the forests back of Lee's army. The soldiers were in fine spirits, and Hooker's proclamation to the army at Chancellorsville on the evening of April 30th, although boastful in tone, did seem to be in agreement with the facts of the situation: "It is with heartfelt satisfaction the commanding general announces to the army that the operations of the last three days have determined that our enemy must either ingloriously fly or come from behind its defenses and give us battle on our own ground, where certain destruction awaits him." It was also reported among the soldiers that Hooker had said he had Lee in such a position that God Almighty could not prevent him from destroying the Confederate army. The Old Testament saying of Ahab to Benhadad comes to mind, when one reads these boasting words of Hooker, "Let not him that girdeth on his harness boast himself as he that putteth it off."

When, a few days later, Hooker led his baffled army back across the Rappahannock to their old encampment, the distress of Lincoln was more poignant than at any time during the war. The conditions were not as bad as Lincoln believed them to be, and the army, as the Gettysburg campaign immediately following demonstrated, was still intact and in splendid military form. But the great expectations of the President and those of the country had again been dashed. Noah Brooks, an inmate of the White House at the time, thus describes Lincoln's anguish of mind: "I shall never forget that picture of despair. He held a telegram in his hand, and as he closed the door and came towards us, I mechanically noticed that his face, usually sallow, was ashen in hue. The paper on the wall behind him was of the tint known as 'French gray', and even in that moment of sorrow and dread expectation I vaguely took in the thought that the complexion of the anguished President's visage was almost exactly like that of the wall. He gave me the telegram and in a voice trembling with emotion, said, 'Read it—news from the army.' (The telegram was from Hooker's chief-of-staff, Butterfield, confirming the rumor that the army had retreated across the river.) The appearance of the President as I read aloud these fateful words, was piteous. Never, as long as I knew him, did he seem so broken up, so dispirited and so ghostlike. Clasping his hands behind his back, he walked up and down the room, saying, 'My God, my God, what will the country say! What will the country say!'"

The next day the careworn President and his military adviser, Halleck, went to visit the army at Fredericksburg, leaving behind them wild rumors that Lee had cut Hooker to pieces and was advancing on Washington, that Hooker was under arrest, Stanton had resigned, and that McClellan was on his way to Washington by special train. This visit contrasted strangely with the former visit when Hooker and the President sat their horses side by side and acknowledged the cheers of the "finest army on the planet."

On his way back to Washington, Lincoln wrote Hooker a letter asking for a new and more successful movement. The letter shows hardly a trace of his anguish of spirit: "The recent movement of your army is ended without affecting its object, except, perhaps some important breakings of the enemy's communications. What next? If possible, I would like another movement early enough to give us some benefit from the fact of the enemy's communications being broken; but neither for this reason nor any other, do I wish anything done in desperation or rashness. An early movement would help to supersede the bad moral effects of the recent one, which is said to be considerably injurious. Have you already in your mind a plan wholly or partially formed? If you have, prosecute it without interference from me. If you have not, please inform me, so that I, *incompetent as I may be,* can try and assist in some plan for the army."

"Some plan for the army." That was what Lincoln was hoping and praying for, a plan that would accomplish something for the cause and the country. He urged Hooker to move soon again, yet in his warning against rashness, betrays the fear that Hooker, baffled and mortified by his reverse, in an effort to retrieve his laurels might lead the army into some desperate adventure, where a worse disaster would befall it. But Hooker, mortified as he must have been, was too much of a soldier to move a great army without any well-defined plan and objective.

In his telegram to Lincoln when he withdrew across the river after the Battle of Chancellorsville, and in a subsequent letter, Hooker explained his action on the ground that after the disaster which befell the right wing of his army, the routing of the 11th Corps, he felt that his chances of success along the line mapped out were so much lessened that it was advisable to withdraw. Thirteen years after the battle Hooker paid a visit to the field of Chancellorsville, and on that occasion said to Samuel Bates, who accompanied him and who asked him why he first halted and then withdrew his army: "We were in this impenetrable thicket. All the roads and openings leading through it the enemy immediately fortified strongly, and it became utterly impossible to maneuver my forces. My army was not beaten. Only part of it had been engaged. The First Corps, led by Reynolds, whom I regarded as the ablest officer under me, was fresh and eager and ready to be brought into action, as was my whole army. But I had been fully convinced of the futility of attacking fortified positions, and I was determined not to sacrifice my men needlessly, though it should be at the expense of my reputation as a fighting officer."

If Hooker, as he intimates in this conversation, and as he said to the President in his telegram and letter, was convinced that a further prosecution of the battle had little chance of success, then he showed moral courage of the highest order in withdrawing. But the student will remember that all but one of his corps commanders, Sickles, a civilian, thought the army ought to stay and fight it out where they were, and that a year later Grant led the army through those same "impenetrable thickets". The rumors that Hooker was drunk during the battle are shown to be false by the direct testimony of Generals Couch and Pleasonton, the former thinking that his unaccustomed abstinence from strong drink was perhaps a reason for the sluggish state of his brain at the critical moments in the conflict.

The real psychology of Hooker's actions during the campaign, when he first faltered, and then withdrew, is the interesting spectacle of the overconfident man suddenly becoming underconfident. This is the explanation of the battle and its results which, according to Major E. P. Halstead, Hooker gave to Doubleday during the Gettysburg campaign. Doubleday said to him, "Hooker, what was the matter with you at Chancellorsville? Some say you were injured by a shell, and others that you were drunk; now tell us what it was." To this Hooker answered good-naturedly, "Doubleday, I was not hurt by a shell, and I was not drunk. For once I lost confidence in Hooker, and that is all there is to it."

If he lost confidence in himself at Chancellorsville, Hooker quickly recovered himself after the battle and kept his army well in hand, the cavalry especially growing bolder and bolder. Some of his chief officers, however, did lose confidence in him, Couch being so disgusted with Hooker's behavior at Chancellorsville that he asked to be relieved from further service in the Army of the Potomac under Hooker. In a letter of May 14, 1863, Lincoln warns Hooker against the disloyalty of his subordinates, saying, "I must tell you that I have some painful intimations that some of your corps and division commanders are not giving you their entire confidence. This would be ruinous, if true, and you should therefore, first of all, ascertain the real facts beyond all possibility of doubt." But of the two most bitter critics of Hooker, Couch and Meade, the former sought service elsewhere, and the latter performed all his duties like the true soldier he was.

As soon as General Lee began the maneuvers which culminated in the invasion of Pennsylvania, Hooker, with keen military intuition, predicted the plan of Lee, telegraphing to Lincoln on June 15th, "It seems to me that he (Lee) will be more likely to go north, and to incline to the west. He can have no design to look after his rear. It is an act of desperation on his part, no matter in what force he moves. It is an act of desperation which will kill copperheadism in the North." No better comment on the military folly of Lee's invasion of Pennsylvania has ever been made, than this of Hooker, uttered almost a month before the Battle of Gettysburg. But in this and in other letters and telegrams it is quite evident that Hooker does not feel the freedom of action which the successful leader of a great army must have, for he says to the President, "I do not know that my opinion as to the duty of this army in the case is wanted; if it should be, you know that I shall be happy to give it." Think of it! A great campaign opening and the commander of the army not sure that his government cares anything about his opinions as to the movements of the army! Much of this feeling on the part of Hooker was due to his conviction that Halleck was not friendly to him. When he succeeded Burnside as commander Hooker made a request of Lincoln that he be permitted to act without undue interference on the part of Halleck, saying that Halleck had opposed his being chosen as commander, and that having been identified with the army in the West he had written and spoken disparagingly of the Army of the Potomac. At the time Lincoln seems to have reassured Hooker, but in the early days of the Gettsburg campaign Hooker's restiveness under Halleck's management again crops out. On June 16th, he telegraphed Lincoln, asking for a closer co-operation, saying of Halleck, "You have long been aware, Mr. President, that I have not enjoyed the confidence of the major-general commanding the army, and I can assure you so long as this continues we may look in vain for success, especially as future operations will require our relations to be more dependent upon each other than heretofore." Hooker felt hampered, as every commander of the army before and after him felt hampered, by the orders of a commanding general who was not himself on the field at the head of the army. It seems strange now that the sagacity of Lincoln did not sooner lead him to abandon the plan under which the war was being prosecuted, and the painful result of which was that in the time of crisis the commander of the army in the field did not feel independent in his movements, indeed, was not sure that his advice was wanted.

In answer to Hooker's telegram Lincoln sent a severe message, settling the question of Hooker's relationship to Halleck: "To remove all misunderstanding, I now place you in the strict military relation to General Halleck as the commander of one of the armies to the general-in-chief of all the armies. I have not intended differently, but as it seems to be differently understood, I shall direct him to give you orders and you to obey them."

This was plain and to the point. But a harsh answer was not in Lincoln's make-up, and on the same day he sent Hooker a kind letter by the hand of Colonel Ulric Dahlgren, afterward to meet death in the raid on Richmond, in 1864. In this letter Lincoln tells Hooker that Halleck has no special fault to find with him save that he writes and telegraphs to the President instead of to the general-in-chief. He pleads with them to be as frank and friendly in their relations with each other as he, the President, is with both, and tells Hooker in closing that from the day Hooker took command of the army until now he had not believed he had a chance to effect anything. But now that Lee has commenced his movement by way of Harper's Ferry, he thinks that Hooker has the chance to destroy him which McClellan let pass in the previous year.

When, on June 5th, Hooker became convinced that Lee was making a move to the north, he telegraphed the President outlining the probable movement of Lee, his head toward the Potomac and the rear at Fredericksburg, exactly as it turned out, and stated that it was his judgmeht that he should "pitch into Lee's rear." At four o'clock that same afternoon Lincoln telegraphed his famous reply in which he advised against the crossing of the river to assail Lee's rear: "If you find Lee coming to the North of the Rappahannock, I would by no means cross to the south of it. If he should leave a rear force at Fredericksburg, tempting you to fall upon it, it would fight in intrenchments and have you at a disadvantage, and so, man for man, worst you at that point, while his main force would in some way be getting an advantage of you northward. In one word, I would not take any risk of being entangled upon the river, like an ox jumped half over a fence and liable to be torn by dogs front and rear without a fair chance to gore one way or kick the other. If Lee should come to my side of the river, I would keep on the same side, and fight him or act on the defense, according as might be the estimate of his strength relatively to my own. But these are mere suggestions which I desire to be controlled by the judgment of yourself and General Halleck."

Five days later, on June 10th, Lincoln telegraphed Hooker repeating his advice against his crossing the river to the south, but suggesting, and

this was the course adopted by Hooker, that if
Lee came towards the upper Potomac that he "follow on his flank and on his inside track. . . . If he
stays where he is, fret him and fret him."

The correspondence between Lincoln and
Hooker during the critical days when it was clear
that Lee was maneuvering for some great thrust,
but just where none knew, makes thrilling reading.
This telegram of June 10th, in which Lincoln advised against Hooker's going south when Lee was
moving north, was in answer to one received
earlier in the day from Hooker. It was a message
which makes the heart leap even after the lapse of
more than half a century, and which must have
stirred the heart of the President, although he at
once wired his counsel against it. It was nothing
less than to cross the Rappahannock and march on
Richmond. Hooker, whose intuition and predic-
tion as to the movements of Lee's army were un-
failingly correct, informed the President that he
thought it was Lee's intention to send a heavy
column of infantry to accompany the cavalry on the
great raid in Maryland and Pennsylvania, and then
added his daring proposal: "I am not satisfied of
his intention in this respect, but from certain movements in their corps I cannot regard it as altogether
improbable. If it should be found to be the case,
will it not promote the true interest of the cause
for me to march to Richmond at once? From there
all the disposable part of the army can be thrown
to any threatened point north of the Potomac at
short notice, and until they can reach their destina-
tion, a sufficiency of troops can be collected to

check, if not to stop his invasion. If left to operate from my own judgment, with my present information, I do not hesitate to say that I should adopt this course as being the most speedy and certain mode of giving the rebellion a mortal blow. I desire that you will give it your reflection." If Lincoln had given his permission and Hooker had marched on Richmond with the consummate skill with which he conducted the march up to the opening of Gettysburg, the capital of the Confederacy must have fallen and the war been finished, for even if Lee had gone on north with Hooker going south, and had taken Harrisburg, Philadelphia, or even Washington, his stay would have been of short duration, and forsaking his prizes he would have been compelled to march back into Virginia with a hostile army waiting for him and a hostile country behind him. But there was in Hooker's bold proposal, as in every great enterprise, a chance of mishap and failure. The anxious President was fearful of any movement that had a chance of failure in it. He was thinking what he afterwards told Sickles he said on his knees to God during the Battle of Gettysburg, that the country could not stand another Fredericksburg or Chancellorsville.

On the 14th of June, when it was well established that the head of Lee's infantry was about Winchester and Martinsburg in the Shenandoah Valley, Lincoln sent Hooker another quaint telegram, saying: "If the head of Lee's army is at Martinsburg and the tail of it on the road between Fredericksburg and Chancellorsville, the animal must be very slim somewhere. Could you not break

him?" But Hooker was keeping his army well in
hand, marching west and north on the inside line
of Lee's march until the army was concentrated
in the neighborhood of Frederick where Hooker
could, as he chose, pass over the South Mountain
and break Lee's long column, or march to strike its
head near Carlisle or Harrisburg. There was, of
course, great concern at Washington and throughout the North, as Lee's advance guard came marching up the Cumberland Valley into Pennsylvania,
but Hooker, Halleck and Lincoln were all hopeful
of a great victory. They felt that Lee, as proved
to be the case, was putting himself in a bad position from which he could extricate his army only
at great loss. Hooker termed it an "act of desperation." Writing to Halleck, with whom he did
little communicating during the campaign, Hooker
said, "I think we may anticipate glorious results
from the recent movement of the enemy whether
he should determine to advance or retreat." Lincoln said to Gideon Welles, on the 26th of June,
"We can't help beating them if we have the man.
How much depends in military matters upon one
master mind! Hooker may commit the same fault
as McClellan and lose his chance. We shall soon
see, but it appears to me he can't help but win."

This hopeful situation was due entirely to
Hooker's masterly handling of the army. Lee's
two objects in going North were to draw Hooker
out where he might turn on him and destroy his
army which had escaped him in the tangles of the
forests about Chancellorsville, and at the same
time threaten and perhaps capture Harrisburg,

Philadelphia or Washington.   But on the 27th of June, despite the panic in Pennsylvania, there was no likelihood of Lee succeeding in either project. Lee's army was spread out through the Cumberland and Shenandoah Valleys, and just on the other side of the mountains, that is, to the east, Hooker's great army, full of fighting spirit and confident of victory, was concentrated in the vicinity of Frederick.   Whether Lee chose to advance or retreat, the Army of the Potomac was in a position to be hurled at him with the certainty of victory, and with the probability of utter destruction of the Confederate forces.   Nothing could have surpassed Hooker's keenness in intuition and skilful handling of the army during those critical days.   This was the situation, when on June 27th, General Halleck, having absurdly refused to let Hooker attach to his army the garrison at Harper's Ferry, Hooker, justly aggrieved, requested to be relieved, and was succeeded by General Meade.

There has been a supposition that Lincoln and Halleck forced Hooker to resign by refusing him reasonable and important requests.   This is based upon the testimony of Charles F. Benjamin, who occupied a confidential post at the War Department and at the army headquarters.   He says that after Chancellorsville, Stanton, Halleck and Lincoln determined that Hooker should not be intrusted with the leadership of the army in another battle.   But in order not to rouse the hostility of the Chase faction in the Cabinet, the removal was postponed until the last hour, and made all the more difficult because of Hooker's splendid management of the army during the march towards Pennsylvania. The correspondence between Lincoln and Hooker gives no indication whatever of such purpose or of a lack of confidence on the part of Lincoln. Reynolds had heard that he was being considered for Hooker's successor and went to the President saying that he would not take the command. He spoke of Hooker's defects, but Lincoln replied, "I am not disposed to throw away a gun because it missed fire once," meaning that because Hooker had not succeeded in his first campaign, Chancellorsville, Lincoln did not intend to abandon him.

Hooker deported himself with great dignity and propriety when he received the midnight call from Meade and Hardie, the purpose of which he did not need to be told. He perhaps did not expect that his request to be relieved would be granted. It must have been with bitter disappointment that he left the army which he had led so successfully, and which was about to commence a battle, which, unless there were terrible blundering, could have no other result but glorious victory. So Hooker passes off the stage of great events.

After Gettysburg Lincoln wrote to Meade, saying, "I have not thrown General Hooker away," and asking if Meade would care to have Hooker as a corps commander. Meade responded in a kind spirit, saying that he would accept Hooker, but would not ask for him. But it was evidently thought better to use Hooker's abilities elsewhere, and he was accordingly dispatched to Chattanooga, where in command of the corps made up of the old

11th and 12th Corps of the Army of the Potomac, he did brilliant fighting under Grant, and in the march to Atlanta under Sherman. But there was ill feeling between Hooker and Sherman, and when, upon the death of McPherson, Sherman made Howard commander of the Army of the Tennessee, Hooker asked to be relieved and his request was granted.

The student of the war will not fail of being impressed with the superb management of Hooker during the maneuvering of the army up to the commencement of the battle of Gettysburg. Meade took over Hooker's staff and merely followed the line of campaign as laid down, for Hooker's positioning of the army made Lee's drawing in of his troops and the subsequent battle inevitable. As the passion and bitterness of the Civil War subside and the historian sees more clearly the men and the measures of the great day, the figure of Joseph Hooker will loom larger than it did in the years immediately subsequent to the war. The resolution of thanks passed by Congress after the battle of Gettysburg gives him his deserved share in that victory and his true place in the history of the war:

"Resolved, That the gratitude of the American people and the thanks of their representatives in Congress, are due, and are hereby tendered to Major-General Joseph Hooker, and the officers and soldiers of the Army of the Potomac, for the skill, energy and endurance which first covered Washington and Baltimore from the meditated blow of the advancing and powerful army of rebels led by General Robert E. Lee, and to Major-General

LINCOLN AND HOOKER

George G. Meade, Major-General Oliver O. Howard, and the officers and soldiers of that army, for the skill and heroic valor which at Gettysburg repulsed, defeated and drove back, broken and dispirited, beyond the Rappahannock, the veteran army of the rebellion."

LINCOLN AND MEADE

Lincoln saw less of Meade and cared less for him than any of the generals whom he appointed to the command of the Army of the Potomac. He was more irritated, more distressed, more perplexed by Meade's management of the army than he was by that of any other commander. Yet it was when Meade was in command that the Army of the Potomac fought the great battle of the war and won its most important victory.

George Gordon Meade was born in 1815 at Cadiz, Spain, where his father, member of an old Philadelphia family, had established himself in business and was also the naval agent of the United States. After preliminary schooling in Philadelphia and at Washington, where he attended the school kept by Salmon P. Chase, afterwards Secretary of the Treasury under Lincoln, Meade was sent to West Point, where he finished number nineteen in a class of fifty-six. He had little liking for the military life and soon found himself engaged in surveys and other engineering works. In the Mexican War he served as a topographical engineer on the staffs of Generals Taylor and Scott. This engineering proclivity clung to him throughout his career, so much so that Grant, in the very generous estimate he makes of Meade, says that "he saw clearly and distinctly the position of the enemy, and the topography of the country in front of his own position. His first idea was to take

GEORGE GORDON MEADE·

advantage of the lay of the ground, sometimes without reference to the direction we wanted to move afterwards."

At the outbreak of the Civil War Meade was engaged in the geodetic survey of the Great Lakes, to which he had been appointed by Jefferson Davis, Secretary of War under Franklin Pierce. He was one of the few officers in the Union army who rose to great distinction during the war who were not resigned from the army when the war commenced. Meade commanded a brigade in the Seven Days' Battle in the Peninsula, and as a commander of a division in Hooker's corps won distinction at South Mountain and Antietam, being made commander of Hooker's corps when the latter was wounded. At the head of his division Meade took part in the futile attack on the Confederate lines at Fredericksburg, and led the Fifth Corps in the Chancellorsville campaign.

When the question of a successor to Burnside was being discussed, Meade's name, together with that of Reynolds and Hooker, was mentioned. He had done nothing that had captivated the imagination of the country as Hooker had, but all associated with him regarded him as a thoughtful and thorough soldier. After the defeat of Chancellorsville a representative of the President waited on General Sedgwick and asked him if, in case there were a change of commanders, he would accept the appointment. Sedgwick refused to consider the tentative offer, but in answer to the question as to the best appointment, said, "Why, Meade is the proper one to command this army."

It is safe to say that after the Battle of Fredericksburg, when it became evident that there would be a change of commanders, Meade's name was before the authorities in Washington. When Lincoln paid a visit to the army at Antietam, shortly after the battle in September, 1862, Meade accompanied him over the battlefield and had the satisfaction of hearing McClellan say to the President, "that there Meade did this and that there Meade did that." The published letters of Meade reveal a singular combination of vanity and humility and show him to be one of the meekest, proudest men that ever lived. When, shortly before the battle of Antietam, General Reynolds was detached from his division for duty in Pennsylvania, and great outcry was made by Hooker and others against his removal, Meade was deeply offended, for since the command of the division devolved upon him, he thought the protest against the removal of Reynolds was a reflection upon his own ability. Again he was jealous of Couch when he was sent to an independent campaign in Pennsylvania. The day before Antietam he wrote to his wife, "I go into the action today as the commander of an army corps. If I survive, my two stars are secure, and if I fall, you will have my reputation to live on."

As a matter of fact, at that time Meade had very little reputation in the country. But coupled with these frequently recurring expressions of pride, and that oversensitiveness which goes with vain natures, there are to be found some of the noblest, wisest and most patriotic of sentiments. The publication by his family of Meade's letters to his wife affords an interesting parallel to the publication of Mc-Clellan's letters to his wife. Both reveal a sincere piety, a genuine love of country and a keen discernment. They also reveal, on the part of Mc-Clellan, a colossal egoism, and on the part of Meade an even more offensive and almost childish vanity, with bitter resentment at what he deemed to be a lack of appreciation of his soldierly qualities or his military successes. Meade was supposed to be the one man who was not ambitious and not striving for high command. Yet in a letter written at the time of Lincoln's visit to the army shortly before the Battle of Chancellorsville, we find this naive comment, showing that Meade too was of like passion with the rest of the army officers, and, we may add, the rest of humanity: "I have attended the other reviews and have been making myself very agreeable to Mrs. Lincoln, who seems an amiable sort of personage. In view also of the vacant brigadiership in the regular army, I have ventured to tell the President one or two stories, and I think I have made decided progress in his affections."

The ill success of Hooker in the Chancellorsville campaign created rather a delicate situation between Meade and Hooker. Meade had a more favorable opinion of Hooker than most of the army officers, nor was he unmindful of the fact that it was at Hooker's earnest representations that he had been chosen to lead his corps when Hooker was wounded at Antietam, and as soon as he took command of the army Hooker made Meade the leader of the Fifth Corps. He was close to Hooker during the Chancellorsville fiasco, and it was to

Meade that Hooker in a moment of despondency said he was almost ready to turn over to him the command of the army, that he had had enough of it and almost wished he had never been born. Three of the generals in the army, Slocum, Sedgwick and Couch, had come to Meade and expressed the opinion that he ought to be placed in command. Under these trying conditions Meade carried himself with dignity and propriety, and the relations between the two men promised well for a time. But Meade had a sharp tongue, and in a confidential interview with Governor Curtin, of Pennsylvania, he severely criticized Hooker's management during the Chancellorsville campaign and the subsequent loss of confidence in him on the part of many of the officers of the army. This conversation was reported in Washington and reached the ears of Hooker, who took Meade to task. Meade gave the explanation of a confidential conversation and the matter was allowed to drop. The final break between the two came when Hooker intimated that his withdrawal across the Rappahannock after the Battle of Chancellorsville was determined by the advice of Meade and Reynolds. Meade regarded this as an effort to make him and Reynolds the scapegoats, and withstood Hooker to his face, telling him that he had made up his mind to withdraw the army before he had consulted any of the corps commanders.

The night of June 26th was a critical one in the history of the Republic. Upon the request of General Hooker to be relieved of the command because of the refusal of the commander-in-chief,

LINCOLN AND MEADE

General Halleck, to give him freedom as to the troops at Harper's Ferry, the Government decided upon the very dangerous policy of removing a popular and, so far as the Gettysburg campaign had proceeded, a very successful commander on the eve of battle. Extraordinary methods were pursued by the Government to transfer immediately the command to General Meade. Armed with duplicate copies of the President's order General James A. Hardie, a personal friend of both officers, in civilian's dress, made his way to Frederick, going first to the tent of Meade. When Meade was awakened and saw Hardie standing over him his first thought was that for some unknown offense Hooker had put him under arrest. When he learned the nature of Hardie's errand Meade became greatly agitated and protested against being placed in command, partly because he had been kept in total ignorance of the movements and disposition of the army, and partly because he thought it an injustice to his close friend, Reynolds, to whom the whole army was looking as Hooker's successor. But the President's order was peremptory. Meade dressed himself and rode with Hardie to Hooker's headquarters, and the army had a new commander. Hooker, keenly disappointed as he must have been, accepted the situation gracefully, and after an affectionate farewell to the troops left for Baltimore.

Just why Meade was selected by the President rather than Reynolds and others, no one will ever know. Halleck suggested he had nothing whatever to do with the appointment, and Stanton probably had considerable influence in the selection. One of the finest chapters in the history of the Civil War and one of the finest tributes to the reach and sway of republican government was the way in which commanders of the army like McClellan and Hooker, both of whom were supposed to entertain the idea that what the country needed in its crisis was a dictator, relinquished their commands when a battle with the enemy was pending, without a word of reproach or revolt, obeying their orders like a private in the ranks. The feeling of relief at Washington at the way in which the army took the removal of Hooker was hardly less than it had been when McClellan was removed.

That the Government realized to the full the unusual action it had taken just as the army was about to move into battle is shown by the order addressed to Meade from Halleck, but undoubtedly inspired by Lincoln. In this letter Halleck said, "You will receive with this the order of the President placing you in command of the Army of the Potomac. Considering the circumstances, no one ever received a more important command; and I cannot doubt that you will fully justify the confidence which the Government has reposed in you. You will not be hampered by any minute instructions from these headquarters. Your army is free to act as you may deem proper. All forces within the sphere of your operations will be held subject to your orders. Harper's Ferry and its garrison are under your direct orders. You are authorized to remove from command any officer or other person you may deem proper. In fine, General, you are intrusted with all the power and authority which the President and the Secretary of War, or the General-in-Chief can confer on you, and you may rely on our full support."

Armed with these extraordinary powers and granted at the very beginning what Hooker had been refused, the authority to direct the troops at Harper's Ferry, Meade assumed the command of the army. With a twinkle in his eye, Meade said to his aide, his son, George, when he stepped out from Hooker's tent, "Well, George, I command the Army of the Potomac!" That was the natural exultation of a man whose ambitions had been fulfilled. But in a more thoughtful mood he wrote to his wife, "You know how reluctant we both have been to see me placed in this position, and as it appears to be God's will for some good purpose— at any rate, as a soldier, I had nothing to do but accept and exert my utmost abilities to command success. This, so help me God, I will do, and, trusting to Him Who in His good pleasure has thought it proper to place me where I am, I shall pray for strength and power to get through with the task assigned me." Thus, humbling himself before Almighty God, the sober and scholarly Meade led his hosts into battle.

In view of the movements of Lee, the army could not have been better positioned than it was, due to the splendid handling of Hooker, who now must see another reap his laurels. At the east entrance to the passes of the South Mountain the army was in a position to break through and fall upon Lee's rear and line of communication west of the mountains, or move into Pennsylvania on the inside of Lee's flank. Hooker had conceived the admirable plan of joining the garrison under French at Harper's Ferry with the corps of Slocum, and having it move up the Cumberland Valley in Lee's rear while the main army moved on the inside track and struck at the head of the column. Had Meade carried out this plan of having a strong body in the rear of Lee, while the main army fought him farther to the north, Lee would have been destroyed. If, after Gettysburg, when Lee retreated towards Hagerstown and the fords of the Potomac at Williamsport, he had been confronted by such a body of troops as Hooker proposed should meet him, the Confederate army would have been annihilated.

As it was, Meade followed out Hooker's general plan, moving north on the inside track of Lee as his legions marched up the Cumberland Valley, and the advance guard towards the Susquehanna River at York and Christiana. Meade had prepared a line of battle at Pipe Creek in Maryland, but the natural course of the march of the army under Hooker's direction made a collision with Lee inevitable, and Lee's westward movement resulted in the conflict on the hills and meadows about the peaceful hamlet of Gettysburg. As Meade had little or nothing to do with the tactics and strategy of the campaign, for Hooker's admirable movements had already determined in a general way the impending conflict, so he had nothing to do with selecting the actual field where took place the clash of arms which shook the world. His advance guard, under Reynolds and Howard, encountered the Confederate advance just to the west and north of Gettysburg. These forces sent back for reinforcements and the great battle was on. Meade did not reach the field until early morning on the 2nd of July, and when he arrived he found the army strongly posted on the hills south of Gettysburg. This line of battle had been chosen by Howard and then strengthened by Hancock, whom Meade had sent ahead to take whatever action he deemed proper. At once Meade saw the strength of the Union position, and chose to stay and fight it out. For that he deserves no particular credit, for even the most unmilitary eye would have taken in the great natural advantage of the position for a defensive battle.

The story of Gettysburg does not fall within the scope of this book. Suffice it to say that Meade fought a careful and courageous battle, though because of his numbers and his position little handling of the army was required. All he had to do was stand against the brave but ill-considered assaults of Lee's infantry. If Meade had fallen on the field of battle on the evening of the third day's fight, when Pickett's men were reeling back towards Seminary Ridge, his fame might have been greater than that of any commander of the Union armies. But fate ruled otherwise. When Hancock was being borne on a litter from the field he sent a penciled note to Meade urging him to make immediately a counter-attack and break the Confederate lines. His chief of cavalry, Pleasonton, begged him to make an assault with the entire army. If he had done so, Lee would have been

crushed and the war ended. But Meade waited
for an hour, a night, a day, another night, and the
next morning Lee was gone. In January of the
same year Meade, commenting on the hesitating
movements of the army under Burnside, had written, "You see, I am among the fire-eaters and may
perhaps jeopardize my reputation by being too decided. But the fact is, I am tired of the playing
war without risks. We must encounter risks if
we fight and we cannot carry on war without
fighting."

If Meade had only remembered that declaration
and acted upon it when Lee was reforming his
beaten army on Seminary Ridge! There was little
risk involved in a general assault upon a half-
shattered army of invaders, far from their base of
supplies, with a range of mountains and a great
river between them and Virginia. But Meade was
not equal to the occasion. Lee was permitted
almost unmolested to withdraw his army, his trains,
his wounded, and his long column of prisoners,
through the passes of the mountains and on to the
Potomac at Williamsport. The very stars in their
courses were fighting against him, for when he
reached the river he found that his pontoon bridge
had been destroyed and the river was so swollen
by the heavy rains that it would be several days
before he could cross.

Meanwhile Halleck and Lincoln were imploring
Meade to strike the final and fatal blow. On July
7th Halleck telegraphed, "You have given the
enemy a stunning blow at Gettysburg. Follow it
up, and give him another before he can reach the

Potomac." Under the same date Halleck forwarded to Meade a message which he had just received from Lincoln, and which read, "We have certain information that Vicksburg surrendered to General Grant on the 4th of July. Now, if General Meade can complete his work, so gloriously prosecuted thus far, by the literal or substantial destruction of Lee's army, the rebellion will be over." On the 8th Halleck telegraphed to Meade, "There is reliable information that the enemy is crossing at Williamsport. The opportunity to attack his divided forces should not be lost. The President is urgent and anxious that our army should move against him by forced marches." On the 12th Meade telegraphed to Halleck that he was getting ready to attack and fight the decisive battle of the war. Yet the precious days went by and the attack was not made.

On the 13th Meade, instead of fighting, held a council of war and reported to Halleck that five out of six of his corps commanders were unqualifiedly opposed to the attack. Therefore he would delay and make more careful examination of Lee's position. To this Halleck responded in a message which must have been inspired, if not dictated, by Lincoln: "You are strong enough to attack and defeat the enemy before he can effect a crossing. Act upon your own judgment, and make your generals execute your orders. Call no council of war. It is proverbial that councils of war never fight. Do not let the enemy escape."

On the 14th Meade telegraphed that that morning he had moved up to attack Lee but found his lines evacuated. What Lincoln and Halleck and the whole nation feared had happened. Lee had recrossed the Potomac and was safe in Virginia. That same day Halleck sent Meade a message still urging him to follow Lee's retreat, but telling him that the escape of Lee's army had "created great dissatisfaction in the mind of the President." Within an hour Meade sent Halleck his request to be relieved, saying, "Having performed my duty conscientiously and to the best of my ability, the censure of the President conveyed in your dispatch of 1 P. M. this day, is, in my judgment, so undeserved that I feel compelled most respectfully to ask to be immediately relieved from the command of this army." Halleck responded that his telegram was not meant for censure but as a stimulus, and refused the application to be relieved. In a private communication of July 28th Halleck speaks kindly and appreciatively of Meade and his leadership of the army, telling him among other things that he had done at Gettysburg that which no other commander of the army had been able to do, brought all his forces into action at the right time and the right place. The President's great disappointment is again referred to with the statement that the President had himself examined all the details of sending every possible reinforcement to the army and that he thought Lee's defeat and destruction were certain. At the close of the letter Halleck reveals the fact that he had recommended Meade to the President for the command of the army at the time of Hooker's removal. In response to this Meade wrote that he did not wonder at the President's disappointment, for he himself was disappointed at Lee's escape, but there was a difference between disappointment and dissatisfaction. Referring to the implied feeling of the President that he had not done all that might have been done, or that another might have done, Meade says: "Perhaps the President was right; if such was the case, it was my duty to give him an opportunity to replace me by one better fitted for the command of the army. It was, I assure you, with such feelings that I applied to be relieved. It was not from any personal considerations, and I have tried in this whole war to forget all personal considerations and have always maintained they should not for an instant influence anyone's actions. Of course, you will understand that I do not agree that the President was right. Had I attacked Lee the day I proposed to do so, and in the ignorance that then existed of his position, I have every reason to believe the attack would have been unsuccessful and would have resulted disastrously."

The distress of Lincoln upon the receipt of the news of the escape of Lee was terrible, greater than at any other crisis in the war. After the adjournment of the Cabinet meeting on the day the news came Lincoln overtook Gideon Welles, Secretary of the Navy, on the lawn and walked with him towards the Army and Navy buildings, telling him that what he had so much dreaded had come to pass and that Lee had crossed the Potomac, and more, that there seemed to him a determination that "Lee, though we had him in our hands, should escape with his force and plunder. And that, my

[179]

God, is the last of this Army of the Potomac!
There is bad faith somewhere. Meade has been
pressed and urged, but only one of his generals
was for an immediate attack, was ready to pounce
on Lee; the rest held back. What does it mean,
Mr. Welles? Great God! what does it mean?"

On the 14th of July, the day that Lee's army
crossed the Potomac, Lincoln wrote to Meade the
famous unsent letter in which he tells why and how
deeply he was disappointed in the escape of Lee,
and what it meant to the cause and the nation:

> I have just seen your despatch to General Halleck,
> asking to be relieved of your command because of a
> supposed censure of mine. I am very, very grateful
> to you for the magnificent success you gave the cause
> of the country at Gettysburg; and I am sorry now to
> be the author of the slightest pain to you. But I was
> in such deep distress myself that I could not restrain
> some expression of it. I have been oppressed nearly
> ever since the battles at Gettysburg by what appeared
> to be evidences that yourself and General Couch and
> General Smith were not seeking a collision with the
> enemy, but were trying to get him across the river
> without another battle. What those evidences were,
> if you please, I hope to tell you at some time when we
> shall both feel better. The case, summarily stated,
> is this: You fought and beat the enemy at Gettysburg,
> and of course, to say the least, his loss was as great
> as yours. He retreated, and you did not, as it seemed
> to me, pressingly pursue him; but a flood in the river
> detained him till, by slow degrees, you were again
> upon him. You had at least twenty thousand veteran
> troops directly with you, and as many more raw ones
> within supporting distance, all in addition to those
> who fought with you at Gettysburg, while it was not
> possible that he had received a single recruit, and

[180]

yet you stood and let the flood run down, bridges be built, and the enemy move away at his leisure without attacking him. And Couch and Smith! The latter left Carlisle in time, upon all ordinary calculation, to have aided you in the last battle at Gettysburg, but he did not arrive. At the end of more than ten days, I believe twelve, under constant urging, he reached Hagerstown from Carlisle, which is not an inch over fifty-five miles, if so much, and Couch's movement was very little different.

Again, my dear General, I do not believe you appreciate the magnitude of the misfortune involved in Lee's escape. He was within your easy grasp, and to have closed upon him would, in connection with our other late successes, have ended the war. As it is, the war will be prolonged indefinitely. If you could not safely attack Lee last Monday, how can you possibly do so south of the river, when you can take with you very few more than two-thirds of the force you then had in hand? It would be unreasonable to expect, and I do not expect (that) you can now effect much. Your golden opportunity is gone, and I am distressed immeasurably because of it.

I beg you will not consider this a prosecution or persecution of yourself. As you had learned that I was dissatisfied, I have thought it best to kindly tell you why.

A week later, in answer to a letter from General Howard, who had written defending the course of Meade, Lincoln wrote as follows:

Your letter of the 18th is received. I was deeply mortified by the escape of Lee across the Potomac, because the substantial destruction of his army would have ended the war, and because I believed such destruction was perfectly easy—believed that General Meade and his noble army had expended all the skill, and toil, and blood, up to the ripe harvest, and then let the crop go to waste.

Perhaps my mortification was heightened because I had always believed—making my belief a hobby, possibly—that the main rebel army going north of the Potomac could never return, if well attended to; and because I was so greatly flattered in this belief by the operations at Gettysburg. A few days having passed, I am now profoundly grateful for what was done, without criticism for what was not done.

General Meade has my confidence, as a brave and skilful officer and a true man.

Colonel Alexander McClure saw Lincoln within a week after the retreat of Lee from Gettysburg and gave him first-hand information about the roads and passes leading from Gettysburg to the Potomac. McClure asked Lincoln if he was not satisfied with what Meade had accomplished. Lincoln answered with his characteristic caution when speaking of the defenders of the Republic, "Now, don't misunderstand me about General Meade. I am profoundly grateful down to the bottom of my boots for what he did at Gettysburg, but I think that if I had been General Meade I would have fought another battle." History confirms the verdict of Lincoln. It is an old military maxim that a retreating army must be given a wall of steel or a bridge of gold. Meade presented Lee with a bridge of gold. Meade was retained in independent command of the Army of the Potomac until Grant arrived on the scene, and under Grant commanded the army to the end of the war. But there is no evidence that Lincoln greatly admired him or expected much of him. When, in March, 1864, Meade asked for a court of inquiry to settle disputes that had arisen about his conduct of the battle at Gettysburg, Lincoln refused in a somewhat curt message in which he told Meade that there was better employment for him and his officers than attending the sessions of a court of inquiry. In his diary for September 21, 1863, Gideon Welles tells of a conversation he had with the President, who at the time was much depressed because of the bad news from Chickamauga. Welles asked him what the immense army of Meade was doing. Lincoln answered that he could not learn that Meade was doing anything or wanted to do anything. "It is," he said, "the same old story of the Army of the Potomac. Imbecility, inefficiency— don't want to do—is defending the capital. Oh, it is terrible, terrible, this weakness, this indifference of our Potomac generals, with such armies of good and brave men." When Welles asked him why he did not remove Meade and choose a better general, the President answered, "What can I do with such generals as we have? Who among them is any better than Meade? To sweep away the whole of them from the chief command and substitute a new man would cause a shock, and be likely to lead to combinations and troubles greater than we now have. I see all the difficulties as you do. They oppress me."

When Grant came east and pitched his tent with the Army of the Potomac, Meade knew that his day was over. Henceforth Grant must increase and Meade must decrease. It was a trying situation for Meade, but he performed his duties with soldierly promptness and obedience. There was nothing in common between Grant and Meade, but Grant entertained a high opinion of Meade's ability. Meade's position with the army was now more like a chief-of-staff than a commander. It was inevitable that he should have dropped out of public notice. When Sherman was made a major-general in August, 1864, Meade felt keenly the omission of his name from the list of promotions. Still more did he resent Grant's giving the independent command in the Shenandoah Valley to Sheridan, who had been very offensive in his conduct to Meade when with the Army of the Potomac. After his victory over Early at Cedar Creek, Sheridan was made a major-general in the regular army. The victor of Gettysburg was still unhonored, and Lincoln must have known of the omission and acquiesced in it. But when Meade was at length appointed to the grade of major-general in the regular army in November, 1864, Grant saw to it that the commission was pre-dated for August, so that Meade ranked Sheridan. In 1866 the rank of General was created for Grant, and Sherman succeeded to the rank of lieutenant-general, thus leaving Meade first in rank among the major-generals. When Grant became President, in 1869, it was generally supposed that Sherman would succeed him as General, and that Meade would become the lieutenant-general. But almost the first official act of Grant as President was to make Sheridan lieutenant-general. This was a terrible blow for Meade, and he stigmatized it as the "cruelest and meanest act of injustice" and expressed the hope that the "man who perpetrated it will some day be made to feel so." Henceforth Meade is as a man whose head is bowed by a great sorrow and who nurses an incurable wound. His contemporaries did not give him the highest rank; nor has history reversed their verdict. He will be remembered as Lincoln wrote to him after Gettysburg—the man who let his "golden opportunity" escape.

LINCOLN AND HALLECK

In Gideon Welles' diary for September 29, 1863, we find this entry: "Halleck, Chase said, was good for nothing, and everybody knew it but the President." That blunt opinion of Chase about Halleck is the one held by nearly every student of the Civil War. He stands out as a man "good for nothing," and that good-for-nothingness recognized by all except the man who called him to his high office and retained him in power to the end of the war. Why did Lincoln not see what all his contemporaries saw? This is one of the puzzles of the war.

No high officer was held in such little esteem by his contemporaries as Halleck. An extraordinary chorus of contempt rises at the mention of his name. To Chase he is "good for nothing"; McClellan, who was quick to recognize ability, says of him, "Of all men whom I have encountered in high position Halleck was the most hopelessly stupid. It was more difficult to get an idea through his head than can be conceived by anyone who never made the attempt. I do not think he ever had a correct military idea from beginning to end." As for the Secretary of the Navy, Gideon Welles, Halleck is his *bête noir*, and every mention of his name and every sight he has of him calls forth an expression of indignation and disgust. Here are some of his thoughts about Halleck: "Halleck is heavy headed, wants sagacity, courage, and heart."

HENRY WAGER HALLECK

LINCOLN AND HALLECK

"Halleck originates nothing, anticipates nothing; takes no responsibility, plans nothing, suggests nothing, is good for nothing. His being at headquarters is a national misfortune." "In this whole summer's campaign I have been unable to see, hear, or obtain evidence of power, or will, or talent, or originality on the part of General Halleck. He has suggested nothing, decided nothing, done nothing but scold and smoke and scratch his elbows. Is it possible the energies of the nation should be wasted by the incapacity of such a man?"

Reading such opinions as these on the part of men who saw Halleck in action, or rather saw him failing to act, the mystery is that Lincoln kept such a man in high office, consulted constantly with him, and deferred to his judgment in military matters. Was there something of worth in the man which Lincoln saw and appreciated, but which escaped the notice of others? However this may have been, no history of Lincoln's relationship to the army leaders would be complete without a chapter telling of his association with Halleck.

Henry Wager Halleck was born in New York, in 1815, graduated from West Point in 1839 and immediately became assistant professor of engineering in the academy. In 1841 he was sent to Europe to study military science and upon his return published a volume under the title *Elements of Military Art and Science*. When the Civil War broke out this book was much used in the training of volunteer officers. In the Mexican War Halleck served with distinction in California. In 1849 he helped frame the constitution of California when it was admitted to the Union. After some years of service in lighthouse and fortification works on the Pacific coast, Halleck resigned his commission and took up the practice of law. In this he was eminently successful. He was also the director of a silver mine and the president of a railway. He was a prolific author, having written besides the work on military science the following books: *Bitumen, Its Varieties and Uses; The Mining Laws of Spain and Mexico; International Law,* and *Treatise on International Law* and *Laws of War;* a translation of Jomini's *Political and Military View of Napoleon,* and also a translation of the work of de Fooz on *The Laws of Mines.* In contrast with Grant, Sherman, Hooker, Sheridan, and other Union generals, Halleck, at the outbreak of the war, was a well-to-do, successful and distinguished man, a scientific soldier, a skilful lawyer, a prosperous business man and an author of note.

It was not strange, therefore, that the aged General Scott began to think of Halleck as his successor at Washington. He was commissioned a major-general on August 19, 1861, and summoned to Washington. But when he arrived there, the affairs in Fremont's department at St. Louis were in such a chaotic state that he was sent west to succeed the "Pathfinder." In the autumn and the winter of 1861 Halleck did a great work of organization. He created and drilled the armies which were shortly to make such a name for themselves in the western campaigns. In a letter to Lincoln in January, 1862, Halleck describes himself "in the condition of a carpenter who is required to build a bridge with a dull ax, a broken saw, and rotten timber. It is true that I have some very good green timber, which will answer the purpose as soon as I can get it into shape and season it a little." This "green timber" he handled skilfully, and ere long it was seasoned well enough to put into the hands of Grant.

One of the great mistakes of the early administration of the war was the creation of three independent commands in the west, under Hunter, Buell and Halleck. Halleck was enough of a soldier to see the danger of this, and repeatedly asked that he be given supreme command. "Make Buell, Grant and Pope major-generals of volunteers," he telegraphed Lincoln the day after the surrender of Fort Donelson, "and give me command in the West. I ask this in return for Forts Henry and Donelson." Lincoln, who had been watching by the bedside of his dying son, Willie, was so overwhelmed with grief that he was reluctant to interfere in the dispute over lack of co-operation between Buell and Halleck. But early in March Halleck secured his desire and the three commands of Buell, Grant and Hunter were put under his direction. Forts Henry and Donelson had already been won; then followed Pea Ridge, Shiloh, Island No. 10, and Corinth. It cannot be said that any one of these victories was due to the ability of Halleck; they were due rather to the initiative and skill of the subordinate commanders. Nevertheless, these armies were under his command, and he authorized the movements and supplied the troops and the munitions of war. Halleck himself did not take the field until just after the Battle of Shiloh, when he supplanted Grant and advanced "with pick and shovel," as Sherman puts it, against Corinth. There he let the splendid army under him lie idle and accomplished little or nothing until Lincoln summoned him to Washington in July, 1862.

With such a record of victories in his department, while in the east no progress was being made, it was but natural that Lincoln and the public at large should have had a very high opinion of the ability of General Halleck. When things commenced to go wrong on the Peninsula under McClellan, Lincoln began to cast about for a man who could devise new plans and co-ordinate the hitherto baffled efforts of the Union armies to put down the rebellion. It was inevitable that he should have thought of the distinguished soldier who had won such laurels in the west. He was supposed, too, to be a man of superior military intelligence, with the mind which could plan and undertake a great enterprise.

Late in June, 1862, when McClellan was on the Peninsula in his campaign against Richmond, Chase, the Secretary of the Treasury and Welles, the Secretary of the Navy, were with the President at the War Department. General Pope was also present. As they were studying the maps which lay on a table Chase said the whole movement upon Richmond was wrong and that nothing could be accomplished until the army was recalled and started for Richmond by the land route, with Washington as the base. "What would you do?"

asked Lincoln of Chase. "Order McClellan to return and start right," responded Chase. Then Pope, looking up, said to Lincoln, "If Halleck were here, you would have, Mr. President, a competent adviser who would put this matter right." How many others suggested to Lincoln that Halleck was the man for the hour we do not know. But we do know that about this time Lincoln made a secret trip to West Point and had a conference with General Scott. In the only record we have of this conference, a memorandum from the hand of Scott, giving the President advice as to McClellan's campaign, there is no mention of Halleck. But it is significant that shortly after this visit Lincoln summoned Halleck to Washington to take the supreme military command. McClellan says that Scott had long wished Halleck to succeed him as general-in-chief and long withheld his resignation so that Halleck might fall heir to his place.

The first intimation we have of Lincoln's purpose to make Halleck the grand marshal of the war is contained in a telegram of July 2, 1862, in which the President says, "Please tell me, could you not make a flying visit for consultation without endangering the service in your department?" On the 6th of July Lincoln writes that he is sending a messenger to Halleck. "He wishes," says the President, "to get you and part of your force, one or both, to come here. You already know I should be exceedingly glad of this if, in your judgment, it could be without endangering positions and operations in the southwest." This messenger was Governor Sprague of Rhode Island. In answer to the proposal which Sprague brought to Halleck from Lincoln, Halleck replied to Lincoln, "Governor Sprague is here. If I were to go to Washington I could advise but one thing—to place all the forces in North Carolina, Virginia and Washington under one head, and hold that head responsible for the result." This must have satisfied Lincoln, for on the 11th of July, 1862, he issued the order, "That Major-General Henry W. Halleck be assigned to command the whole land forces of the United States as general-in-chief, and that he repair to this capital as soon as he can with safety to the positions and operations under his charge."

The coming of Halleck to Washington as commander-in-chief was fraught with disaster for the Union armies in the east. But in the west it had one very important and fortunate effect, for Grant, next in rank, now succeeded to the command of Halleck's department. The appointment of Halleck was well received by the country, and it must be remembered that the adverse comments on his ability are related with his career at Washington and not with what had gone before.

Writing at the time of Halleck's appointment to the supreme command, General Sherman says of him, "General Halleck was a man of great capacity, of large acquirements, and at the time possessed the confidence of the country, and of most of the army. I held him in high estimation, and gave him credit for the combinations which had resulted in placing this magnificent army of a hundred thousand men, well equipped and provided, with a good base, at Corinth, from which he could move in any direction."

Gideon Welles in his diary for September 3rd, lets us behind the political scenes at Washington, when he says, "The introduction of Pope here, followed by Halleck, is an intrigue of Stanton's and Chase's to get rid of McClellan. A part of the intrigue has been the withdrawal of McClellan and the Army of the Potomac from before Richmond and turning it into the Army of Washington under Pope." (Welles means the Army of Virginia, not the Army of Washington.) There is no doubt about an intrigue to get rid of McClellan, but that Stanton had much to do with bringing Halleck to Washington is not likely, for McClellan says that a day or two before Halleck arrived in Washington Stanton came to caution him against Halleck, saying that he was "probably the greatest scoundrel and most barefaced villain in America," that he was totally destitute of principle, and that in the Alameda Quicksilver case he, Stanton, had convicted Halleck of perjury in open court. McClellan adds that when Halleck arrived he came to him and warned him against Stanton, saying of Stanton almost precisely what Stanton had said of Halleck. Plainly, there was not much love lost between the two.

The day after he arrived in Washington Halleck went to McClellan's headquarters on the James River and consulted with him about future plans. The upshot was that Halleck advised and then finally ordered McClellan to withdraw his army. Just how far Halleck was responsible for this great military blunder is not clear. His advice might have led the Government to maintain McClellan where he was, but it is plain that the Government was fully determined in its own mind to withdraw McClellan from the Peninsula before Halleck arrived on the scene. Once he had acquiesced in the plan to bring McClellan back and unite his army with that under Pope, Halleck ought to have seen that the thing was done with dispatch. But he allowed McClellan to discuss and delay until Lee fell on Pope before the Army of the Potomac was united with him. . At the very beginning of Halleck's stay as commander-in-chief Lincoln was doomed to disappointment, for it was plain that Halleck was the last man in the world to assume the heavy responsibility of directing the armies which were engaging in battle almost at the gates of the capital. What a picture of incompetence, of lack of aggressiveness and fighting heart it is that Halleck presents during the fateful days of the Second Battle of Manassas, when at length, after having ignored and snubbed McClellan, he finally telegraphs him, "I beg of you to assist me in this crisis with your ability and experience. I am entirely tired out!" Early on the morning of the 2nd of September, 1862, Halleck and Lincoln went together to the home of McClellan in Washington and besought him to resume command of the forces about Washington. In the first crisis which had arisen Halleck had failed, failed dismally and completely. Yet, as we shall see, he survived this, and many another, failure.

As his relationships with McClellan had been unfortunate so also they were with McClellan's successor, Burnside. At a meeting of the Cabinet, when the possible successor to McClellan was being discussed, Mr. Bates suggested that Halleck take command of the army in person. "But the President," writes Welles in his diary, "said, and all the Cabinet concurred in the opinion, that Halleck would be an indifferent general in the field, that he shirked responsibility in his present position, that he, in short, is a moral coward, worth but little except as a critic and director of operations, though intelligent and educated." After Burnside had made his ghastly failure before Fredericksburg he advised Lincoln to remove both Stanton and Halleck, saying that neither of them had the confidence of the army. When Burnside was contemplating another crossing of the Rappahannock, Lincoln, fearful lest a new disaster should befall the army, and perplexed as to how he should counsel Burnside, wrote the following impatient letter to his commander-in-chief:

My dear Sir: General Burnside wishes to cross the Rappahannock with his army, but his grand division commanders all oppose the movement. If in such a difficulty as this you do not help you fail me precisely in the point for which I sought your assistance. You know what General Burnside's plan is, and it is my wish that you go with him to the ground, examine it as far as practicable, confer with the officers, getting their judgment and ascertaining their temper—in a word, gather all the elements for forming a judgment of your own, and then tell General Burnside that you do or that you do not approve his plan. Your military skill is useless to me if you will not do this.

Halleck responded to this letter by sending in his resignation. But Lincoln, his exasperation now in subsidence, spoke encouragingly to Halleck and refused to accept his resignation. The copy of the letter to Halleck bears the following endorsement in Lincoln's hand, "Withdrawn because considered harsh by General Halleck."

When Hooker succeeded Burnside as commander of the Army of the Potomac the first thing he asked for was freedom of action without being hampered or hindered by Halleck. By this time Halleck was considered as an obstacle to the success of the generals in the field. The President promised Hooker a free hand, and in the subsequent campaigns of Chancellorsville and on the march towards Gettysburg, Hooker communicated directly with Lincoln, ignoring the commander-in-chief. That he could have done this shows that Halleck's position was only nominal. In reality, he was a sort of chief-of-staff, or military adviser, to Lincoln. As the campaign which culminated in Gettysburg progressed, Hooker became more and more convinced that Halleck was blocking him, and made definite complaint to Lincoln. To this Lincoln answered: "I believe Halleck is dissatisfied with you to this extent only, that he knows that you write and telegraph to me. I think he is wrong to find fault with this; but I do not think he withholds any support from you on account of it. If you and he would use the same frankness to one another, and to me, that I use to both of you, there would be no difficulty. I need and must have the professional skill of both, and yet these suspicions tend to deprive me of both."

That this critical situation had arisen in the management of the army as it was marching toward the invading foe was due to no one but Lincoln himself, for it was he who had permitted Hooker at the beginning to take a thoroughly unmilitary procedure in ignoring the commander-in-chief. Lincoln's perplexity over the relationship of Hooker and Halleck came to an end with Halleck's foolish refusal to let Hooker withdraw the garrison from Harper's Ferry. This was followed by Hooker's resignation, and Meade was appointed to the command of the Army of the Potomac.

Not only was Halleck useless in the planning of military movements, but even as go-between, or chief clerk, acting for the President and the War Department, he exasperated the commanders of the armies in the field. This was true in his relationship with McClellan, Burnside, Hooker, Sherman, and Rosecrans, and with Grant, too, when Halleck commanded in the west, although Grant had no complaint to make of Halleck's support during the Vicksburg campaign. Halleck had an interesting clash with General Rosecrans. In March, 1863, there was a vacancy in the rank of major-general, in the regular army, and General Rosecrans, along with other officers, was being pressed for the vacancy. Thinking to get some action out of the army commanders, Halleck addressed a letter to the generals being named in connection with the honor, and said the vacancy would be given to the general in the field who should first win an important and decisive victory. Unquestionably this suggestion of Halleck's has a Lincoln note about it, nor is it at all likely that he would have sent such a letter unless the President had at least seen it and given his approval. None of the other officers who received the letter took exception to it, but the fiery Rosecrans thought it an insult to his honor, and sent an angry reply saying, "As an officer and a citizen I feel degraded to see such auctioneering of honor. Have we a general who would fight for his own personal benefit, when he would not for honor and country? He would come by his commission basely in that case, and deserve to be despised by men of honor."

A month or two later Halleck again roused Rosecrans by intimating to him that he was using the telegraph too freely for the report of insignificant events. This drew from Rosecrans a fierce rejoinder in which he said that he regarded the insinuation of Halleck as "a profound, grievous, cruel, and ungenerous official and personal wrong. If there is any one thing I despise and scorn, it is an officer's blowing his own trumpet or getting others to do it for him. I had flattered myself that no general officer in the service had a cleaner record on this point than I have. I shall here drop the subject, leaving to time and Providence the vindication of my conduct, and expect justice, kindness, and consideration only from those who are willing to accord them." Rosecrans was noted for his irascibility; but making due allowance for that, Halleck's dealing with him was irritating in the extreme. Thus did Halleck, unable to help his generals or plan for them, splendidly succeed in provoking them to wrath.

Gideon Welles in his diary refers contemptuously to the report that Halleck was engaged in some literary work. Colonel Lyman in his *Meade's Headquarters, 1863-1865,* throws more light on this literary enterprise of Halleck, and does so by quoting the picturesque language of Benjamin Butler. When Butler was in command on the James, Halleck had sent him an aide without consulting him. When the aide made his appearance at Butler's headquarters Butler said to him, "Aide-de-camp, sir! Ordered on my Staff, sir! I'm sure I do not know what you are to do. I have really nothing for you. All the positions are filled. Now there is General Halleck, what has *he* to do? At a moment when every true man is laboring to his utmost, when the days ought to be forty hours long, General Halleck is translating French books at nine cents a page; and, sir, if you should put those nine cents in a box and shake them up, you would form a clear idea of General Halleck's soul!"

During the period of Meade's command of the army Halleck did little more than transmit the requests or orders of Lincoln. Had he been a real commander-in-chief, he would have issued peremptory orders, or gone himself in person to the front and seen that Meade attacked Lee before he withdrew across the Potomac after Gettysburg. But as it was he sent only polite requests to Meade to move against Lee. Grant, who had so unfortunate an experience with Halleck when he was under his command in the west, has nothing but praise for

Halleck's loyal support of him during the Vicksburg campaign. It was Halleck who solved the difficult problem of Grant in relationship to McClernand and the quasi-independent command which Lincoln had unadvisedly allowed him in the campaign against Vicksburg, by giving Grant full authority to take command of the operations in the field and to relieve McClernand whenever he thought it for the good of the cause. When Grant came to Washington as supreme commander Halleck was made chief-of-staff, the post that he had really been filling all the time he had been at Washington. With Grant at the head of affairs, Halleck's importance was now quite secondary. When Early made his famous threat against Washington, and property was destroyed near Baltimore and Washington, the Postmaster-General, Blair, whose place in the suburbs of Washington had been destroyed by Early's soldiers, made slurring remarks about the incapacity and cowardice of the defenders of the city. These sarcastic flings of Blair so stung and outraged Halleck that he wrote to the Secretary of War a letter in which he wished to know "whether such wholesale denouncement and accusation by a member of the Cabinet receives the sanction and approbation of the President of the United States? If so, the names of the officers accused should be stricken from the rolls of the army; if not, it is due to the honor of the accused that the slanderer should be dismissed from the Cabinet." Stanton forwarded the letter to the President who at once answered him as follows:

LINCOLN AND HALLECK

Sir: Your note of today inclosing General Halleck's letter of yesterday relative to offensive remarks supposed to have made made by the Postmaster-General concerning the military officers on duty about Washington is received. The general's letter in substance demands of me that if I approve the remarks I shall strike the names of those officers from the rolls; and that if I do not approve them the Postmaster-General shall be dismissed from the Cabinet. Whether the remarks were really made I do not know, nor do I suppose such knowledge necessary to a correct response. If they were made, I do not approve them; and yet, under the circumstances, I would not dismiss a member of the Cabinet therefor. I do not consider what may have been hastily said in a moment of vexation at so severe a loss is sufficient ground for so grave a step. Besides this, the truth is generally the best vindication against slander. I propose continuing to be myself the judge as to when a member of the Cabinet shall be dismissed.

On the same day the President read to the Cabinet when it convened this bit of advice: "I must myself be the judge how long to retain in and when to remove any of you from this position. It would greatly pain me to discover any of you endeavoring to procure another's removal, or in any way to prejudice him before the public. Such endeavor would be a wrong to me, and, much worse, a wrong to the country. My wish is that on this subject no remark be made nor question asked by any of you, here or elsewhere, now or hereafter."

This lecture to the Cabinet was anent the strong opposition which had arisen in the country against the Postmaster-General, Montgomery Blair, Halleck's complaint being only one of a great number.

LINCOLN AND HIS GENERALS

In September Lincoln asked for the resignation of the troublesome, but patriotic and loyal, Postmaster-General. Blair resigned without a quarrel, and worked ardently for the re-election of Lincoln.

When Lincoln was laid low by the assassin's bullet Halleck was one of the group who stood about his bed in the 10th Street house as the President breathed his last, and heard Stanton exclaim, "Now he belongs to the ages!" The strange thing is not that Lincoln should have chosen Halleck for commander-in-chief in the summer of 1862, for many of the best military minds and the sentiment of the people at large approved the choice. The strange thing is that after his incapacity had been so strikingly demonstrated Lincoln should have kept him in command and constantly deferred to his judgment. Originating nothing, taking no responsibility in times of danger or crisis, letting the burden rest on the shoulders of other men, afraid to make use of the powerful weapon that Lincoln had placed in his hands when he made him the supreme commander of the armies of the Union, Halleck is a contemptible, almost ridiculous figure. One would laugh at him, were it not for the fact that his incompetence was one of the chief factors in the repeated and tragic reverses which befell the Union armies. Selected by Lincoln and kept in power by Lincoln, Halleck did more injury to the cause of the North than any other man. "Good for nothing," as Chase put it, "and everybody knew it but Lincoln."

LINCOLN AND GRANT

On a warm June day in 1861, a modest looking man of about forty years of age made his way out from Springfield, Illinois, to the fair grounds, where a number of volunteer regiments from that state were being drilled. He had neither sword nor uniform, the stick in his hand and the red bandana about his coat being the only signs of authority. The regiment to which he had been assigned, the 21st Illinois volunteers, was composed of turbulent, insubordinate troops, who had already driven their colonel away from the camp. Before this stranger took over the command of the regiment, John A. Logan, representing Governor Yates, and a famous political speaker, made the soldiers an oration. At the close of the speech the men began to shout for Grant to address them. He did so, but with characteristic brevity, saying, "Go to your quarters!" The unruly regiment had found its master. But no one on that day could have predicted that within less than a year this unheard-of and discredited captain from the old army would be one of the chief figures of the war, the most successful general of the west, and that in less than three years Lincoln would call him to Washington to command all the armies of the nation. Fremont, McClellan, McDowell, and other well-known officers were already major-generals. But the man upon whom Lincoln would at length rely to put down the rebellion was

this travel-stained captain with the red handker-
chief about his waist, a stick in his hand.

Grant was made a brigadier-general soon after
he entered the service of the nation, but Lincoln
probably knew little or nothing about him until
after the capture of Forts Henry and Donelson, in
February, 1862. Donelson gave Grant his chance
and he made the most of it. The victory which he
won there was the first ray of light that Lincoln
had seen, and the whole nation rejoiced in the
triumph. Grant's terms to Buckner had been "Unconditional Surrender," and playing with Grant's
initials, the country fondly referred to him as
"Unconditional Surrender" Grant.

But even as he tasted victory and popular
esteem the cup of bitterness was not far from
Grant's lips. His first difficulty arose with the
irritable and fault-finding Halleck, then in command in the Mississippi Valley. Halleck, displeased
at Grant's meagre reports of what he was doing,
and at some independent moves he had made in
following up the Confederate army, had complained
to McClellan at Washington that Grant would not
answer his messages. McClellan then wired that
Grant be relieved from duty and the charges
against him investigated. He also authorized Halleck to put Grant under arrest. Halleck directed
him to turn over the command of the expedition
up the Tennessee River to General C. F. Smith and
remain himself at Fort Henry. Grant did so, and
immediately asked to be relieved. Fortunately
Halleck, when all the facts were known, saw that
he had no cause to complain of Grant's course,

ULYSSES S. GRANT

and restored him to the command. "Thus," writes Grant, "in less than two weeks after the victory at Donelson, the two leading generals in the army were in correspondence as to what disposition should be made of me, and in less than three weeks I was virtually in arrest and without a command." But Grant's difficulties with his superiors after Donelson were only a prelude to the storm of popular execration that broke over his head after the Battle of Shiloh.

Shiloh was the first great battle of the war, and it was not until then that the country began to realize what a grim and bloody business war is. But the people were not prepared for the casualties that began to come in after the battle. The sober verdict of history is that although at Shiloh Grant displayed in a magnificent manner those qualities of calmness and doggedness and holding on with full confidence of victory, which were to serve the nation so well in many a future campaign, his positioning of his army was faulty in the extreme, and it was the fine fighting spirit of the soldiers which saved the army on the first day's battle rather than anything done or ordered by Grant or the other generals on the field. The battle ended with a most important victory for the North. But the thunder of the cannon in the great fight in the solitudes of Shiloh had hardly died away before reports began to flow into Washington about Grant's mismanagement and incapacity. There were ugly rumors, too, of his drinking to excess. An echo of those rumors is heard in the telegram which Stanton sent to Halleck after the Battle of Shiloh, asking about the battle and saying the President was anxious to know if the heavy losses were due in any way to Grant's mismanagement or incapacity. General Halleck, in command of the department, joined the army on the march towards Corinth, and Grant was made second in command, a position where he had rank but no authority. The situation was intolerable to him and he asked to be relieved from duty. General Sherman, who also was an object of the popular anger about Shiloh, relates in his letters the clamor against Grant and how it nearly resulted in the country losing his services: "He (Grant) is as brave as any man should be, he has won several victories such as Donelson which ought to entitle him to universal praise, but his rivals have almost succeeded through the instrumentality of the press in pulling him down, and many thousands of families will be taught to look to him as the cause of the death of their fathers, husbands, and brothers. Grant had made up his mind to go home. I tried to dissuade him, but so fixed was he in his purpose that I thought his mind was made up and asked for his escort a company of the 4th Illinois. But last night I got a note from him saying he would stay. He is not a brilliant man, but he is a good and brave soldier, tried for years; is sober, very industrious, and as kind as a child. Yet he has been held up as a criminal, a drunkard, tyrant and everything horrible."

In his memoirs Sherman adds a little more to the interesting story of how he helped to save Grant for the army. Upon going to visit him at his headquarters he found him all packed and ready to start in the morning. Grant told him that he felt he was in the way and could stand it no longer. Sherman begged him to stay, illustrating his argument by his own experience, how he had been declared crazy by the press of the country and was ready to quit and resign, but a single battle had given him new life. He told Grant that if he went away events would go right along but he would be left out; whereas if he remained, some happy accident might restore him to favor and his true place. Grant then promised to wait for a little, and said he would not leave without first communicating with Sherman. Grant remained with the army and in a short time the "happy accident," the appointment of Halleck as commander-in-chief at Washington, left Grant in command of the army.

We know now that a more powerful factor than Sherman's intercession or Grant's own patience under abuse was at work, saving him for the army and the cause. That factor was Lincoln's sagacity and his faith in Grant. The storm of popular denunciation threatened for a time to sweep Grant out of his command, whether he wished to stay with the army or not. He was bitterly assailed for being absent from his command when the first day's battle at Shiloh started, and it was openly said that only the gallantry of the troops and the timely arrival of Buell with the Army of the Ohio upon the scene of conflict saved the day for the Federal army. The Grant who after Donelson had been hailed as the Man of Destiny, was now denounced as an incompetent winebibber. About the only man in Congress who espoused the cause of Grant was his firm friend, Elihu Washburne, from Illinois. The strength of the popular demand for Grant's removal may be judged from the fact that Colonel Alexander McClure, who had no personal feelings against him and was not sure that he was unfit for the command in the west, was yet convinced that the administration dare not retain him in face of the strong adverse sentiment in the nation. In his concern McClure went to Washington and had a midnight conference with Lincoln in which he urged the President to remove Grant for the good of the cause. He pressed upon the care-worn President the immediate removal of Grant as "an imperious necessity to sustain himself." Lincoln listened in silence, his feet resting on the top of the marble mantel. None understood better than Lincoln the importance of the popular sentiment in a democracy at war. When McClure had finished his appeal, Lincoln gathered himself up in his chair and said in a tone of great earnestness, "I can't spare this man; he fights!" It was Lincoln who saved Grant for the army and for the great career which now rapidly opened before him.

The most influential Democrat in Illinois was John A. McClernand. When war came McClernand, like Douglas, lost no time in letting his loyalty to the Union be known. Lincoln was ever ready to recognize and honor Democrats of this kind and McClernand was rapidly advanced in rank until he was a major-general. He was patriotic, brave, dashing, but without capacity as a general. After Shiloh he had visited Washington and secured from Lincoln permission to raise a corps of troops in the middle west for the purpose of opening up the Mississippi, with the understanding that he was to have the command of the expedition. Before he could bring his troops to the front Grant had sent Sherman against Vicksburg in the unsuccessful assault at the bluffs of the Yazoo River. There McClernand joined him with his own corps and assumed command of the expedition. But Grant was determined that McClernand, in whose ability as a general neither he nor the other high officers had any confidence, should not lead the move against Vicksburg. The matter was solved by Grant himself going to the front and taking command of the army in the field. This was a mortal offense to McClernand, who felt that Grant was depriving him of the post that had been specially created for him by Lincoln. From the very opening of the Vicksburg campaign until near its successful close McClernand's conduct was trying in the extreme to Grant. But he did not dismiss him from the army until there appeared in the newspapers a congratulatory order of McClernand to the men of his corps claiming all the credit for the recent success of the Federal army. This was too much for Grant and he immediately relieved him. When General James H. Wilson read him Grant's order relieving him, McClernand looked up and exclaimed, "Well, sir, I am relieved!" Then after a pause, "By G——, sir, we are both relieved!" What he probably meant was that his passing from the army would mean the passing of Grant, too. But if that was his purpose he was unable to make good the threat. He very soon, however, had his influential friends at work in his behalf and they addressed a letter to Lincoln in August asking that McClernand be restored to the command of his corps or that he be given an independent command. Lincoln was manifestly embarrassed, for he undoubtedly had given McClernand to understand that he was to lead the troops in the expedition down the Mississippi. At the same time he was more than pleased with the great achievement of Grant and would do nothing to hamper or annoy him. This feeling of embarrassment comes out in the letter Lincoln wrote to McClernand in response to the appeal of his friends. In this letter Lincoln writes: "I doubt whether your present position is more painful to you than to myself. Grateful for the patriotic stand so early taken by you in this life-and-death struggle of the nation, I have done whatever has appeared practicable to advance you and the public interest together. No charges, with a view to a trial, have been preferred against you by anyone; nor do I suppose any will be. All there is, so far as I have heard, is General Grant's statement of his reasons for relieving you. And even this I have not seen or sought to see; because it is a case, as appears to me, in which I could do nothing without doing harm. General Grant and yourself have been conspicuous in our most important successes; and for me to interfere and thus magnify a breach between you could not but be of evil effect. For me to force you back upon General Grant would be forcing him to resign. I cannot give you a new command because we have no forces except such as already have commanders. I am constantly pressed by those who scold before they think, or without thinking at all, to give commands respectively to Fremont, McClellan, Butler, Sigel, Curtis, Hunter, Hooker, and perhaps others, when, all else out of the way, I have no commands to give them. This is now your case; which, as I have said, pains me not less than it does you. My belief is that the permanent estimate of what a general does in the field is fixed by the 'cloud of witnesses' who have been with him in the field and that, relying on these, he who has the right needs not to fear."

During the long Vicksburg campaign the popular discontent with Grant began to break out once more. The old stories about his drinking were revived and a clamor arose for his removal. Grant refers to this in his *Memoirs* where he says: "Because I would not divulge my ultimate plans to visitors they pronounced me idle, incompetent, and unfit to command men in an emergency, and clamored for my removal. I took no steps to answer these complaints, but continued to do my duty, as I understood it, to the best of my ability." In order to keep in close touch with the army about Vicksburg, Stanton resorted to the rather unusual procedure of sending down Charles A. Dana to stay at headquarters and send frequent reports on the commander, his generals, and the condition of the army. Grant found in Dana a loyal friend and the reports which he sent back to Washington confirmed the faith which the administration had reposed in him.

When the great news came of the fall of Vicksburg, Lincoln sent Grant a fine congratulatory letter in which he said:

My dear General: I do not remember that you and I ever met personally. I write this now as a grateful acknowledgment for the almost inestimable service you have done your country. I wish to say a word further. When you first reached the vicinity of Vicksburg, I thought you should do what you finally did—march the troops across the neck, run the batteries with the transports, and thus go below; and I never had any faith except a general hope that you knew better than I that the Yazoo Pass expedition and the like could succeed. When you got below and took Port Gibson, Grand Gulf and vicinity, I thought you should go down the river and join General Banks, and when you turned northward, east of the Big Black, I feared it was a mistake. I now wish to make the personal acknowledgment that you were right and I was wrong.

Almost a month later, August 9th, at the end of a letter to Grant, Lincoln says, "Did you receive a short letter from me dated the thirteenth of July?" This was a reference to the letter of congratulation after Vicksburg, and reveals the fact that for a month at least Lincoln's fine letter had gone unanswered. But this did not provoke Lincoln so long as Grant turned in victories. In a letter to Burnside written about the same time, and in reference to Grant having promised to send Burnside at Cincinnati the 9th Corps, Lincoln alludes to Grant's slowness as a correspondent and says, "General Grant is a copious worker and fighter, but a very meagre writer or telegrapher." In Lincoln's letters to Grant after Vicksburg, and they had almost no correspondence before that, there is always the recognition of Grant as a successful commander, and a tone of deference to his wishes and plans. The fatherly, guardianlike way in which Lincoln had been accustomed to write to his generals, urging them to do this or that, or to avoid this or that peril, is abandoned, and Lincoln writes to Grant as the man who knows how to organize victory. From Vicksburg clear down to the fall of the curtain at Appomattox, "God bless you!" is the frequent expression of Lincoln's communications to Grant.

There was considerable criticism of Grant's course in paroling the prisoners taken at Vicksburg, it being feared that many of them would find their way back into the ranks of the Confederate armies. This undoubtedly happened. But as an effective force Pemberton's army was destroyed. In defending the course of Grant Lincoln reverted to one of his favorite anecdotes, that of Sykes and his yellow dog. "Sykes had a yellow dog he set great store by, but there were a lot of small boys around the village, and that's always a bad thing for dogs, you know. These boys didn't share Sykes' views. Even Sykes had to admit that the dog was getting unpopular; in fact, it was soon seen that a prejudice was growing up against that dog that threatened to wreck all his future prospects in life. The boys after meditating how they could get the best of him, finally fixed up a cartridge with a long fuse, put the cartridge in a piece of meat, dropped the meat in the road in front of Sykes' door and then whistled for the dog. When the dog came out he scented the bait, and bolted the meat, cartridge and all. The boys touched off the fuse with a cigar, and in about a second a report came from that dog that sounded like a clap of thunder. Sykes came bouncing out of the house and yelled, 'What's up? Anything busted?' There was no reply except a snicker from the small boys roosting on the fence; but as Sykes looked up he saw the whole air filled with pieces of yellow dog. He picked up the biggest piece he could find, a portion of the back with a part of the tail still hanging to it, and after turning it round and looking it all over, he said, 'Well, I guess he'll never be much account again—as a dog.' And I guess Pemberton's forces will never be much account again—as an army." Lincoln related this story to Grant in their first private interview at Washington.

So far as their correspondence shows, the only time Lincoln and Grant came into collision with one another was in January, 1863, when Grant, annoyed by Jewish peddlers in the army, issued an order expelling from his department all Jews. This order was immediately revoked by Lincoln.

Grant's success at Vicksburg, followed by the brilliant victories about Chattanooga, in November, 1863, made him the pre-eminent military figure of the war. Congress recognized this leadership by restoring the grade of lieutenant-general. Lincoln then sent in Grant's name to the Senate and he was confirmed the second day of March, 1864. On the 8th day of March, 1864, a brown-bearded man of forty-two, accompanied by a lad of fifteen, stepped up to the desk at the *Willard Hotel* in Washington and wrote on the register, "U. S. Grant and son, Galena, Ill." That same night Grant went to the reception at the White House, where he was immediately the center of all eyes. In order that he might be seen by the guests and acknowledge their cheers, Grant somewhat awkwardly mounted a sofa. In the private interview which followed Lincoln related to him the Sykes "dog story," and with this characteristic introduction began to talk about the plans for the future. The President, knowing his diffidence as a speaker, gave him a copy of the remarks he would make when he handed him his commission on the following day, and suggested to Grant that in his speech of acceptance he might say something which would tend to obviate any jealousy towards him on the part of the other generals of the army and also a word or two which would put him on as good terms as possible with the Army of the Potomac.

The next day the commission was formally presented to Grant by Lincoln, who said, "General Grant, the nation's appreciation of what you have done, and its reliance upon you for what remains to be done in the existing great struggle, are now presented, with this commission constituting you lieutenant-general in the Army of the United States. With this high honor devolves upon you, also, a corresponding responsibility. As the country herein trusts you, so, under God, it will sustain you. I scarcely need to add that, with what I here speak for the nation, goes my own hearty personal concurrence."

To this Grant responded as follows: "Mr. President, I accept the commission, with gratitude for the high honor conferred. With the aid of the noble armies that have fought in so many fields for our common country, it will be my earnest endeavor not to disappoint your expectations. I feel the full weight of the responsibilities now devolving on me; and I know that if they are met, it will be due to these armies, and above all, to the favor of that Providence which leads both nations and men." The reader will note that Grant in his speech of acceptance made no reference to the two matters the President had asked him to introduce.

At a subsequent interview Lincoln told Grant that he had "never professed to be a military man, or to know how campaigns should be conducted, and never wanted to interfere in them: but procrastination on the part of the commanders, and the pressure from the people of the North and Congress, which was always with him, forced him into issuing his series of military orders, one, two, three, etc. He did not know but that they were all wrong, and he did know that some of them were. All he wanted or had ever wanted was someone who would take the responsibility and act, and call on him for all the assistance needed, pledging himself to use all the power of the government in rendering such assistance." But Lincoln always had some plan in mind for his armies and proceeded to tell Grant what it was. He produced a map of Virginia and pointed out two streams which empty into the Potomac, and suggested that the army might be moved by boats and landed between the mouths of these streams. Supplies could be brought up by the Potomac and the two tributary streams would serve to protect the Union flanks when the army moved out. Grant says that he listened respectfully, "but did not suggest that the same streams would protect Lee's flanks while he was shutting us up."

Lincoln's rejected plan for the new campaign was probably the last effort of the President along that line. Henceforth the burden of the military responsibility rested upon the shoulders of Grant. Lincoln had at length found a man after his own heart, one who would "take the responsibility and act." Both Halleck and Stanton gratuitously and impertinently warned Grant not to divulge his plans to Lincoln, for he was so kind-hearted that someone would be sure to get it out of him. Grant said nothing to Lincoln about his plans, neither did he communicate them to Stanton or Halleck. On April 30, 1864, just before the great campaign of the east and the west opened, Lincoln wrote Grant a sort of farewell letter in which he expressed his full confidence, and said he would not ask for the particulars of his plans, but did say that he was "very anxious that any great disaster or capture of our men in great numbers shall be avoided." At their last interview before the Army of the Potomac crossed the Rapidan into the Wilderness, Grant explained to Lincoln how it was necessary to have a very large number of troops to guard and hold the territory which had already been captured and prevent incursions into the Northern States, and that these troops could do this work as effectively by advancing as by remaining still, for by advancing they would compel the enemy to keep detachments to hold them back.

This was the idea back of Grant's plan of a general movement of the troops on all fronts. Lincoln replied, "Oh, yes! I see that. As we say out West, if a man can't skin, he must hold a leg while somebody else does."

Then followed the plunge into the Wilderness and the fearful fighting by day and the weary marches by night until Grant reached the James River and commenced where McClellan had left off three years before. During these anxious days Lincoln and Grant had little communication. Grant was too busy fighting to write and Lincoln left him to his own devices. After the ghastly repulse at Cold Harbor, on the 3rd of June, the cry of "Grant the Butcher!" went up in the North, the spirits of the populace sank, and there were all the premonitions of another storm of popular wrath against Grant. But Lincoln bowed his head before the blast and let it blow over, confident that Grant would take Richmond as he had promised to do when they had first met. As the two armies struggled desperately with one another in the tangles of the Wilderness, Grant sat whittling and smoking beneath the trees, but with the will to victory written in every line of his face. After every battle, no matter what the result, the order was always "Advance!"

After Grant's army had established itself about Petersburg, Lincoln went down to City Point to visit him. The President presented an odd appearing as, mounted on Grant's big bay, "Cincinnati," he rode through the ranks. He wore a high silk hat and a frock coat, soon covered with dust, and his trousers worked up far above his shoetops. Grant suggested that they ride over to visit the colored troops of Smith's corps, who had made such a gallant assault on the Petersburg redans a few days before. Lincoln expressed his delight, saying that the gallantry of the colored troops had vindicated him in his advocacy of raising colored regiments. A wild scene ensued as Lincoln reached the camp of the negroes. The black men came cheering and singing and weeping about him and greeted him as the Angel of the Lord. Commenting on the bravery of the black troops Lincoln said to Grant, "I think, General, we can say of the black boys what a country fellow said when he went to a theatre in Chicago and saw Forrest playing Othello. He was not very well up in Shakespeare, and didn't know that the tragedian was a white man who had blacked up for the purpose. After the play was over the folks who had invited him to go to the show wanted to know what he thought of the actors, and he said, 'Waal, layin' aside all sectional prejudices and any partiality I may have for the race, derned ef I don't think the nigger held his own with any on 'em.'"

In the fall of 1864 the October elections in Pennsylvania had gone against the Republican party. There could be no doubt about the victory in the national elections in November, but there was the fear of a weakened prestige for the administration if Pennsylvania and New York should go Democratic. McClellan, native son, was the Democratic candidate, and a vigorous campaign was being conducted by his managers in the state. McClure had another midnight conference with Lincoln at the White House. When the subject of the forthcoming election was introduced the President said, "Well, what's to be done?" McClure suggested that as Grant's army was quiet before Petersburg, and Sheridan's beyond Winchester, 5,000 Pennsylvania soldiers be furloughed from each army and sent home so that they might vote.

Lincoln's face brightened at the suggestion. Then McClure added, "Of course, you can trust Grant to make the suggestion to him to furlough 5,000 Pennsylvania troops for two weeks?" To his surprise a shadow fell upon Lincoln's face and he was silent. McClure exclaimed, "Surely, Mr. President, you can trust Grant with a confidential suggestion to furlough Pennsylvania troops?" Lincoln still was silent, evidently distressed. After a minute or two of silence, McClure said, "It can't be possible that Grant is not your friend; he can't be such an ingrate?" After a little hesitation Lincoln answered, "Well, McClure, I have no reason to believe that Grant prefers my election to that of McClellan." When he recovered from his anger and astonishment, McClure told the President that Meade was a soldier and a gentleman, and that an order to him would be sufficient. Lincoln answered, "I reckon that can be done."

McClure, thus warned about Grant, said to Lincoln, "What about Sheridan?" At that the sad face of the President lightened up and he exclaimed, "Oh, Phil Sheridan; he's all right!" The troops were sent home and swelled the Republican majority to 14,364.

LINCOLN AND GRANT

When Grant was retiring from the Presidency McClure met him at Drexel's bank in Philadelphia and sounded him out as to his feelings towards Lincoln and McClellan during the election of 1864. Grant responded that it would have been obviously unbecoming on his part to have given a public expression against a general whom he had succeeded as commander-in-chief.

Whatever may be said today about Grant's attitude during the election, the fact remains that one of the sorrows and burdens of Lincoln's heart was that he could not feel that his chief general cared greatly whether he was victorious or not in the contest with McClellan. Truly he was a man of sorrows and acquainted with grief. McClure thinks that Grant was at fault in never in any way recognizing the debt of gratitude which he owed to Lincoln for retaining him in command in the west when the popular clamor against him was so strong. The election of 1864 gave him a chance to do this, but he did not avail himself of it. Even the most scrupulous will be inclined to think that Grant could have taken a little more interest in Lincoln's re-election without in any way compromising his position as commander of the army, especially since McClellan had been nominated by a convention which had declared the war a "failure". Grant had described himself as "by no means a Lincoln man," referring to the political campaigns in the west before the war. On the other hand, Lincoln may have mistaken Grant's reticence for an indifference which did not exist.

On March 20, 1865, Grant telegraphed the President, "Can you not visit City Point for a day or two? I would like very much to see you, and I think the rest would do you good." Lincoln accepted the invitation and arrived on the 24th, bringing with him Mrs. Lincoln and their youngest boy, "Tad"; the eldest son, Robert, was now a member of Grant's staff. Grant sensed the collapse of Lee's army, the fall of Petersburg and the capture of Richmond and wanted Lincoln to be in at the death. The President was in great good humor and regaled the officers at headquarters with his anecdotes. It was during this visit that he had the famous interview with Grant, Sherman and Porter on board the *River Queen*. Referring to his recent meeting with the Confederate Commissioners at Hampton Roads, Lincoln asked Grant if he had noted the enormous overcoat which Alexander H. Stephens, a very small man, was wearing. Grant said that he had. "Well," said Lincoln, "did you see him take it off? Didn't you think it was the biggest shuck and the littlest ear that ever you did see?" Grant afterwards related this to General Gordon, who in turn told Stephens, much to the latter's delight.

As they sat one night about the campfire Lincoln in his anecdotal method was prophesying that England would regret the stand she had taken during the war, illustrating his point with the story of a western barber who, in order to get at the beard of a hollow-cheeked man, thrust his finger in the man's mouth and pressed out the cheek. But in a careless moment he cut through the man's cheek and into his own finger. At the end of this parable,

LINCOLN AND GRANT

Grant looked up and said, "Mr. President, did you at any time doubt the final success of the cause?" "Never for a moment," was the reply of the President as he leaned forward in his camp chair and raised his hand by way of emphasis.

When Petersburg was taken Lincoln gave Grant an affectionate greeting at his headquarters in the captured town and said to him, "Do you know, General, I had a sort of sneaking idea all along that you intended to do something like this: but I thought sometime ago that you would so maneuver as to have Sherman come up and be near enough to co-operate with you." Grant replied that he had concluded it would be better to let the Army of the Potomac deliver the finishing blow to Lee's army, for if the army under Sherman was even near the scene of surrender, the old cry about the superiority of the western troops would be raised and it would be claimed that they had won the war.

After entering Richmond amid the tears and cheers of the negroes, Lincoln returned to Washington. There on the fatal Friday, April 14th, Grant met with Lincoln and the Cabinet. Grant expressed some anxiety as to Sherman's situation, not having heard from him for some time, but Lincoln then assured Grant that good news would soon come in, for on the night before he had dreamed the dream which had always preceded great events. In a strange vessel he was rapidly approaching a dark shore. This dream he had had before Antietam, Murfreesboro, Gettysburg, and Vicksburg. Grant responded that Murfreesboro was no victory and had no important results. But the President insisted that the dream was the precursor of great news from Sherman, for he knew of no other important event pending.

But another great event was at the door, and that night it would enter to shock the world, although neither Lincoln nor any of his advisers was conscious of its near approach. Lincoln invited General Grant and Mrs. Grant to accompany him and Mrs. Lincoln to the theatre that night. Grant said they would go if in the city, but if his other matters could be attended to he planned to leave Washington that night and go to visit his children, who were in school at Burlington, N. J. On the way to the station that night Grant was shadowed by a man who had frightened Mrs. Grant by his close scrutiny at the hotel during the day. When the photographs of Booth were published they at once recognized him as the man who had shadowed them. When taking the ferry at the Delaware River, at Philadelphia, Grant received the telegram announcing the assassination of Lincoln and hurried back to Washington. Some time after the assassination he received an anonymous letter saying that the writer had been selected by Booth to board Grant's train at the station in Washington and kill him. The conductor had refused him entrance and he was thankful that he had thus been spared committing a murder.

United in their great labors for the salvation of the country, it was only by one of those little chances upon which great issues turn that Grant and Lincoln were not united in death at the assassin's hand. Grant's last message to Lincoln was when he spoke at the dedication of the great obelisk at Springfield, when he said, "From March, 1864, to the day when the hand of the assassin opened a grave for Mr. Lincoln, the President of the United States, my personal relations with him were as close and intimate as the nature of our respective duties would permit. To know him personally was to love and respect him for his great qualities of heart and head, and for his patience and patriotism. With all his disappointments from failures on the part of those to whom he had intrusted commands, and treachery on the part of those who had gained his confidence but to betray it, I never heard him utter a complaint, nor cast a censure for bad conduct or bad faith. It was his nature to find excuses for the his adversaries. In his death the nation lost its greatest hero; in his death the South lost its most just friend."

Three score and four years have passed since the beginning of the Civil War. But even so, we are still too near to that stirring epoch to say with assurance how many of its chief actors will have an abiding place in the history of the nation. It is quite likely that a century hence some of the men dealt with in this book will be not even names. But of this at least I think we can be sure: Lincoln and Grant belong to history. Their names and their fame are secure. Whoever else shall be forgotten, they will be remembered as long as it shall please God to give America a name and a place among the nations of the earth.

[END]

AUTHORITIES

The chief mine of information concerning the American Civil War is the great collection of orders, reports and findings known as the War Records, and published by a generous and grateful Government. But in addition to this priceless collection there has arisen a vast literature of a more personal nature. Nearly every chief figure of the Civil War has written a book, or had a book written about him. For the purpose of my investigation such books as the *Personal Memoirs of U. S. Grant, Memoirs of W. T. Sherman,* McClellan's *My Own Story, Butler's Book,* by General Ben Butler, McClure's *Lincoln and Men of War Times,* Gideon Welles' *Diary,* etc., have proved very helpful. I have consulted, too, the many excellent biographies of the generals of the war, personal letters, and such classics of the Civil War literature as Nicolay and Hay's *Lincoln,* John C. Ropes' *Story of the Civil War,* and the notable series of papers, *Battles and Leaders of the Civil War.* In addition to this wide range of written sources, it has been my very great pleasure and rare privilege, during the years of my study, to talk with the survivors of the great conflict, both officers and soldiers. What an opportunity this has been can be appreciated if one stops to reflect that ten years hence the veterans of the Civil War will be seen no more on our streets. From this rich oral tradition I was able to learn much that had not been written in books.